THE MAKING OF A *Funeral Director*

JANICE J. RICHARDSON

CANADA

THE MAKING OF A FUNERAL DIRECTOR

ISBN 978-0-9952395-4-8
eISBN 978-1-7713639-6-9
ASIN B015P9ZYCE

Printed in Canada

First Printing, 2017

2nd Edition

Cover image – Janice J. Richardson
Cover design – Deana, Graphic Genius & MJ Moores, Infinite Pathways

9 8 7 6 5 4 3 2 1

WHAT PEOPLE ARE SAYING ABOUT

THE MAKING OF A *Funeral Director*

"Both entertaining and informative. [As] a young widow I would have been honored to have Ms. Richardson as a funeral director. She shows compassion in her words and demonstrates her unwillingness to ever give up. My hat is off. Not many could endure what she did and turn it into the fuel she needed to follow her dream."

~ *Barb T.*

"A great read. As a funeral director myself, I can recommend anyone thinking of funeral service as a career to read this or if you are just interested in our wonderful profession, it is really informative.

~ *Carl*

"Amazingly frank, thorough and a pleasure to read. I thank the writer for her honesty and memorable stories of the business."

~ *Kelly M.*

"One of the most heartfelt, honest, and real stories to come across my desk in years. Richardson doesn't pull her punches as she opens her soul to the world. You don't need to be a funeral director to fall in love with the trials this woman went through to be able to follow her heart ... and her calling!"

~ *MJ M.*

Other Books by Janice J. Richardson

Spencer Funeral Home
Niagara Cozy Mysteries

Casket Cache
Winter's Mourning

Coming Soon
Grave Mistake

TABLE OF CONTENTS

THE MAKING OF A *Funeral Director*

INTRODUCTION

The day after the murder the headlines read "Homicide Suspect Arrested." It was just one more murder in Toronto. My partner and I received a call to go to the scene just before midnight. We responded promptly, within the hour, as is expected in coroner's cases.

My partner left his vehicle a few blocks from the scene and rode in with me. Upon arrival at the address, we were waved through the police line and directed to the house. The area was alive with activity, police, media and a crowd of onlookers watching at the barricade. An officer escorted us inside where a detective in a white disposable coverall me us.

"Where are your AIDS suits?" he asked.

"We don't have any," I replied. "They aren't issued, we'll just have to be careful."

"There is a lot of blood," he stated and led us down the hall.

The victim lay on the kitchen floor face down, partially decapitated. A puddle of blood spread out from the body for several feet. "We know this victim had AIDS," said the officer.

"When did he die?" I asked.

"Around noon today," was the reply. It is known that the AIDS virus can live for hours, even days.

"Don't you even have boots?" the officer asked. My partner and I looked at each other and shrugged.

"Just gloves," we replied.

The police photographer asked for a few more minutes to finish before we transferred the body. We removed our jackets and rolled up our sleeves in preparation. Since it was a crime scene we could not put our jackets down nearby. One of the officers standing by took them outside to the porch. As soon as he opened the door the media lights flooded the entrance, then just as quickly shut off again once they realized it wasn't the removal team.

The officer snorted, "They've been here for five hours waiting for you people." We stood and chatted with the detective while waiting for the photographer to finish. He related the details of the murder, a rather grizzly one. The police had a suspect and expected to make an arrest quickly.

'When the photographer finished, we were given permission to step in. The floor was slippery and we moved carefully and deliberately.

"May I move this chair please?" I asked the identification officer.

"Just a sec," he replied and he stepped in a chalked around the chair legs.

"OK, would you mind rolling him over so I can get some pictures," the ID officer said. That meant hiking up my skirt, tucking it as tightly as possible and taking a deep breath to try to block the smell of the blood and not slip and fall in the puddle.

Carefully my partner and I rolled the victim over and held our position. It was quite uncomfortable, both of us were doing our best to ensure we didn't brush the bloody floor or touch the body other than with our gloved hands. The photographer worked as quickly as possible, fully aware of our discomfort.

"OK, done," he finally said. "He's all yours." The detective gave us permission to remove the deceased. Slowly and cautiously we covered the victim's hands with paper bags and transferred the body to the pouch we had opened on the stretcher near us. Since the victim had been mutilated and it was important we did not add to the damage.

The officers stood by quietly and watched. We stripped off our gloves, put them inside the pouch and belted the body tightly to the stretcher. We had stairs to navigate on the way out and we did not want any movement of the body. The detective placed a police seal on the pouch A young constable retrieved our jackets and escorted us to the door. This time the media left their lights and cameras on.

"Ready?" my partner asked.

"Let's go!"

"How do I look?" he asked.

"Photogenic and handsome as always," I teased. Both of us disliked the wall of cameras we had to face from time to time, and hated seeing ourselves on the news. In my case, since I carried the lighter end of the stretcher, it was always my back end to the camera.

As we proceeded out the door several officers walked with us. One of them placed his hand in the small of my back and walked down the stairs with me, a gesture I truly appreciated. Klutzy by nature, my balance walking backwards and downwards was tenuous at best. My partner was momentarily blinded by the lights and we took our time.

We loaded the stretcher in my vehicle. The young constable hopped into the seat beside me and my partner walked back to his car. We pulled away, looking straight ahead.

A few minutes later he spoke, snapping me out of my reverie. "I could give you a ticket for that," he said.

"What? What did I do?"

"You just ran a stop sign," he said seriously.

"Oh no, I didn't – did I?"

No reply.

"Really?"

"Yep."

"Oh shoot. I was lost in thought I didn't see it." I laughed weakly. "Guess you hear that excuse all the time. I was just thinking about this call."

I had been deep in thought however, wondering how I had come to this in such a short period of time. Had you told me a year previously that I would be living and working in Toronto doing coroner's calls I would have laughed.

"I'll let you off with a warning this time," he said with mock seriousness and added "How can you do this job?"

I glanced over at the young man and smiled. "Because I want to be a funeral director. What better training ground? Besides, it beats being shot at."

He chuckled.

"Let me ask you the same question – what made you decide to become a police officer?"

We exchanged our stories all the way to the Coroner's Office – two people who obviously enjoyed their work and didn't mind talking about it.

This is the story of one funeral director in training. It could be the story of any funeral director. For the most part we follow similar paths to get our licenses. The events in this story are true, and with one exception, changed slightly to protect the families of the deceased.

CHAPTER ONE

My Mother Works with Dead Things

Life is mostly froth and bubbles
Two things stand like stone
Kindness in another's troubles
Courage in our own.

-Gordon

Grief will come to all of us. Most of us know what grief means – few know all that it means. It was the grieving process that awakened in me the desire to become a funeral director. Only the person involved can know her/his own grief, no one else can really share it. Simple kindness can do more to ease pain than good intentions and lofty words. My grief lasted for months. It took months to come to fruition.

Five years before, in 1985 I launched a secretarial business. In retrospect, I had more enthusiasm than brains, but that enthusiasm was hard to dampen. It sustained me through those hard years. I read somewhere that one of the biggest problems with success is that its formula is often the same as that for a nervous breakdown – seventy hour weeks, no days off, no vacations.

My husband and children bore it patiently because the end justified the means. Or so I rationalized. A major setback mushroomed and the resulting stress and frustration ended my dream. I crawled under my desk two days before Christmas and started to whimper. Several hours later I was admitted to the psychiatric ward and over Christmas and New Year's I mourned the loss of the business in hospital.

In the months following my discharge I continued to grieve. Physically and emotionally I no longer had the energy or drive to carry on. Positives became negatives, what I had once viewed as challenges became annoyances. I could no longer live below the poverty level, deal with difficult clients and manage staff, demanding creditors or the labour-intensive work. For nine months I grieved, not caring if I ever worked again.

To change careers in my mid-thirties was a difficult prospect. But to have continued in the business was impossible too. Faced with major insecurity and lacking the emotional energy to move forward I made an appointment at the university counselling service. They provided vocational testing and I was at a loss as to what to do. At my insistence, the psychologist agreed to do a Weschler Adult Intelligence Test. All my life I had wanted a university degree. I hoped the Weschler would give me the concrete evidence that I was capable of getting one, not wise enough at the time to know that a degree would not make me a better person.

He agreed to do the Weschler on the condition that I complete several other tests and compare results – the Myers-Briggs (a personality profile) and the Strong Campbell Inventory of Vocational Skills.

During the chat prior to discussing the test results he asked me what career I wanted to pursue. If I could be anything I wanted – what would it be?

My answer surprised him as much as me. I don't quite know where it came from, but there was no hesitation.

"A funeral director," I blurted. Once the words left my mouth, I knew I had set a new course and a weight lifted from my soul.

We then reviewed the tests. The results were interesting. I learned that although I was capable of university, I scored poorly in tests that required global thinking. On the other hand, I enjoyed facts and absorbed them like a sponge.

The Myers-Briggs provided the most useful results. I was surprised to discover that I had a tendency toward introversion, preferring to use my senses rather than my intuition. It showed a strong tendency to judge, something I was not proud of. One of the suggested careers for the personality profile I fit was that of a mortician. The vocational test did not give me an answer, grief and depression had affected the outcome of that test.

Since the response of "funeral director" popped out of my mouth so easily I did some memory searching. As a child my parents did not hide reality from me, preferring to expose me to life in all its' best and worst. Consequently, I attended relatives' funerals from a very young age.

When I was eight I recall clearly attending an uncle's funeral. I remember watching the funeral home staff closely. I recalled the smell of the funeral home and the flowers and the quiet solemn hallways and suites. I wanted to know how they got the body into the casket, why they used so much makeup and why my uncle's body was so cold.

I recall asking my mother why they didn't warm him up. I enjoyed the solemnity and dignity of the service and clearly remembered standing at the graveside, the sun filtering through the trees as the funeral director leaned over and reverently spread sand on the casket (you know – earth to earth, ashes to ashes, dust to dust). I didn't equate it with a cross at the time. I remember thinking to myself, "someday I'm going to do that."

As is my nature, once I told the psychologist funeral service was an option I researched the educational process with the tenacity of a pit bull. In our province thirty percent of the funeral directors were female. I was aware that a neighbouring province had only one female director.

I called Humber College, the only English-speaking funeral service education program in Ontario, and spoke with the program coordinator, Don Foster. It was a two-year program, one year of study, a year of apprenticeship with a consolidation before the Board exams.

He explained there had been three hundred and twenty applicants for one hundred and twenty positions the previous year. The screening process was stringent and in spite of careful selection, the attrition rate was thirty-three percent. The courses were challenging, the hours of work long, and apprenticeships in parts of the province non-existent.

In order to pursue my dream I would have to leave home, find a job, a place to live in Toronto and still send money home to my family while attending school full time. Student loans were not readily available at that time.

Once my mind was made up I just had to sell the idea to my family. My husband, a laid-back gentle soul, took it all in stride. He always encouraged me to do my best and even when I failed he never said "I told you so."

My youngest child who had special needs didn't really understand. As long as she was safe, loved and fed it didn't matter to her. Her world was secure.

My fourteen-year-old daughter was a different story. She was mortified. My attempts to explain what being a funeral director involved fell on deaf ears. She imagined zombies and horror movies. She was totally grossed out and would say to anyone who would listen, "my mother works with dead things." I had yet to set foot in a funeral home, but she repeated her mantra to anyone who would listen.

As part of my preparation for college I decided to test the academic waters by enrolling in a summer school biology course at a senior matriculation level in high school. Six hours a day of class, then off to work for a few hours, an hour's drive home and homework. In high school I had not taken science courses. In grade 9 I failed physical education, the resulting 49% mark in that course caused me to lose my entire year. In the late sixties it meant that instead of taking a 5 year academic program I was required to move to a 4 year secretarial course, changing the course of my entire life.

The biology course was an eye-opener. I had absolutely no idea what a polypeptide chain or a covalent bond was. Mitosis? Dominant and recessive genes? As the course progressed (actually it was more like a few days into the course) I was sure there was something wrong with me. My classmates were all in their late teens and were taking the summer course to boost their marks for university or pass the course if they failed. They were light-years ahead of me. I had the lowest mark in the class ten days into the course and I started to panic.

Every spare minute was spent studying and working on my midterm paper. I had a lot to learn about research, taking over twenty hours to produce a five-page essay. The biography was almost as long as the paper. I would study in the bathtub and glance at my notes on the car seat beside me at stop lights. When I started biology, I didn't factor in chemistry – the periodic table was an enigma. That biology course proved to be by far the most challenging educational pursuit to date.

The day we wrote the final exam I did my best. Generally, I like exams and tests when I'm prepared, anxiety isn't an issue.

Leaving the final, I leaned up against the lockers and slid to the floor with my mouth hanging open. The teacher had taken the time to get to know her students at the beginning of the course. She'd given me every encouragement and knew my plans.

Our marks were available that afternoon. My future hinged on whether or not I could pass a science course. My final grade – 73%, the term paper pulled me through. Driving home, tears of relief flowed freely and I alternately laughed and cried.

The next step was to tackle more courses to match the objectives of the Funeral Service Education program in order to reduce my course load. The Nursing Program at our community college offered Anatomy and Physiology, Microbiology, Pathology and Nursing Communications (a therapeutic approach to interviewing). Somehow, I just assumed I could take those courses if I simply paid for them.

When I was informed by the Registrar's Office that I had to be enrolled in the nursing program to take nursing courses I went to the top. I explained to the Dean my desire to enter Funeral Service. He was sympathetic and waived the rules.

My first class was Anatomy and I loved it. My hard work paid off and my grade reflected my effort. Communications and microbiology were equally as exciting. I was on my way.

One of the prerequisites for admission to the Funeral Service Education Program at Humber is a forty-hour observation period in a funeral home.

I didn't know any funeral directors in our area, so I picked a funeral home at random and telephoned for an appointment.

The director and I discussed the objectives of the observation period and what it means to be a funeral director. By this time some of my misconceptions had been challenged. I was surprised by the complexities of the job. The business of death was starting to be discussed outside the industry, changing the traditional to a simplified version of a funeral service. I tend to view funeral service as a business. If it is not a well-run business then professional services, at whatever level the family chooses, cannot be performed.

The director graciously agreed to accept me for the forty-hour period. I had written several papers in the nursing courses on grief facilitation and the effect of the funeral on the grief process and how to utilize effective therapeutic communication. But I had yet to darken the door of a funeral home. It had been years since really viewing a dead body closely.

While it is relatively easy to get the education, it has to translate into the real world and I was eager to see if I could meet the challenge. Academic meets reality. He invited me to work a visitation that evening and asked me to come in early to get acquainted.

As I entered the funeral home I was struck by the quiet solemnity. The air was cool and smelled faintly of cleaning supplies. The place was immaculate. There was no one in sight but I could hear a vacuum cleaner running. I stood for a minute appreciating the décor and the muted soft colours. It felt restful and comfortable.

Finally, I went down the hall and peeked into a room, startling the funeral director who had been vacuuming. It flashed through my mind that someone else on staff should be doing the cleaning. It wasn't long before I fully understood the role of teamwork in the job, no one should be above menial tasks.

Over coffee, the director and I reviewed the course outline and he explained what I was to do that evening. You could say I started at an entry level position, I was to open the door. He showed me around the main floor and lounge, we made coffee and I took my position.

As people entered I greeted them pleasantly, not "good evening" but "hello". It's not a good evening if you have lost a family member or friend. If there were several visitations as is common in larger funeral homes, then it would be followed by "can I help you" or "who are you here to see" and they would be directed to the appropriate suite.

I had practiced the "benign" look that many directors seemed to have. As I got to know the directors better, the "benign" look caused some merriment. It was easy for them to go from laughter to a genuinely sympathetic demeanor when a family arrived. It wasn't easy erasing my face in a flash, it took practice.

The funeral director had taken the time to explain donations and phone lines earlier, so he excused himself and went downstairs to the preparation room, leaving me with another director.

About an hour later, that director remarked that I seemed to be handling things well and that he was going home. Off he went, leaving me with a suite full of visitors coming and going, the lounge and coffee, phone lines and donations. I knew I could buzz the director who was downstairs if I needed help.

I was curious about the preparation room but it was off limits to me at that point and I didn't even know where it was or how to find it. It was well-hidden and locked away. The evening flew by and three hours later when the director emerged from below I was hunting for light switches to close up. In retrospect, I should have let him know when the family was leaving as it was customary for the managing director to greet them upon arrival and say goodnight as they left.

He was surprised to find out I'd worked alone, but I reassured him that I would have buzzed for help had I been stumped. He then asked if I wanted to observe the funeral the next day.

Did I! He then took me to the suite and asked me to help. Walking over to the casket which had been closed for visitation he lifted the lid and instructed me to hold it up. He carefully removed the ring and glasses, stating the family had requested them.

I studied the body. My first impression was the same as it was many years ago, that it looked too made up. I have a friend who never thinks the deceased looks "lovely", to her that isn't a concept, her view is that they just look dead. She's right of course, but until you lose someone you love, the preparation and casketing can make a difference in their appearance.

Other than my first impression I didn't bat an eyelash as the funeral director adjusted the deceased's hands. I did feel a rush of relief as I headed home – so far, so good.

The funeral service was held in the funeral home chapel. I arrived an hour early, appropriately attired in black, grey and white. I took my post at the door. The funeral cars pulled up and I met the drivers. The director in charge asked me to place something in the funeral coach. That was the first time I had heard that term and I didn't have the foggiest idea which car it was.

I wandered over to one of the drivers stating, "This has to go into the funeral coach," and watched as he went to the hearse. Sneaky, but at least I didn't look as stupid as I felt, and now I knew.

I directed people to the chapel trying to look suitably benign. The funeral director seated the family and the pallbearers while the organist played on and on…and on. The minister had not yet arrived. By this time, the funeral director was pacing up and down the sidewalk outside and one could feel the stress radiating from him.

I recalled the conversation with the Program Coordinator at Humber when I asked him about funeral directors leading services. “It can be done,” he’d replied. “But it’s not a common occurrence.” I wondered which funeral director would be brave enough to try.

The phone chime broke the tension, it was the wayward minister who was lost. Rather than give him directions, the limo driver fetched him and the service began a wee bit late.

During the service the funeral directors stood outside the chapel watching through the curtain like actors waiting for their cue. At the end of the service they took their place and led the pall-bearers to the coach. The director pulled me aside and asked me to stop traffic on the street so the procession and cars could proceed.

Feeling a little foolish I stood at the curb and watched for his signal at the front of the procession. When he nodded, I stepped onto the street, held up my arm, willing the traffic to stop. I squeezed my eyes shut. Much to my relief, the cars on the road did stop and I waved the cars in the parking lot forward once the lead car, family car and coach started. I pointed to the headlights of the cars that had not turned their lights on.

Once the procession was underway I mustered my dignity and strode back to the curb.

“Quite a little power trip,” I muttered to myself as I headed into the funeral home to prepare for the post-funeral reception. I changed into a different outfit, something businesslike and a bit less funereal.

When the family returned from the cemetery their mood was noticeably brighter. I stood at the counter pouring coffee and tea and serving food. There were smiles and subdued laughter. Several young men (pallbearers) stood nearby chatting with me. As the conversation became easier, one of them asked a question. “Why do they only lower the casket partway and why do they take the flowers to the grave?”

Thinking I was the last person they should be asking, I came up with what I thought would be an appropriate response. “It’s too hard on the family to lower it all the way down,” speaking more from a cultural perspective than with clinical knowledge. “And the flowers add some brightness to a very sad situation. The committal is so final.”

They continued to chat with me for the rest of the reception, so they must have been satisfied with the answer. I learned something from them too, first exposure to a funeral can be befuddling.

During the reception there was no sign of the funeral directors, their job was completed. Basically, their presence ended with the committal.

As I started cleaning up I was aware of how exhausted I was, not used to be being on my feet for hours left me drained. The funeral director wandered into the room to forage for leftovers. He glanced around and praised my work. He watched me clean up while I watched him clean up the leftovers. His next remark completely caught me off guard.

“Would you like to go on a transfer?”

“Sure!” was my quick, enthusiastic response, my sore feet and fatigue forgotten. We headed to the garage and checked the vehicle to ensure it was ready to pick up the deceased. One of the other directors followed us to the garage and warned me not to drive with him. We left laughing.

As we drove to the hospital though, I was thinking about the morgue. As a medical secretary I’d heard stories from the interns and residents about their first time at autopsy or in the morgue. I was no superwoman – was I going to disgrace myself and faint too? The funeral director was all business at the hospital, signing for the death certificate and morgue key, exchanging pleasantries with the admission clerk. We wound our way back to the vehicle which was parked at the back of the hospital in a secluded area, removed the stretcher and headed down the hall to the morgue.

The morgue resembled a walk-in freezer and cold air rushed out as we entered. Stretchers were lined up, most empty. There was a plastic sheet somewhat shaped like a body directly in front of us. I took a deep breath as the director checked the tag on the toe. He also lifted the plastic to double check the wrist band, then moved the stretcher into the hall. Parking the hospital stretcher next to the one we brought he explained how to move a body.

"So far so good" I thought to myself, thankful that I wasn't queasy or dizzy.

"How do you move a body when you are by yourself?" I asked him, think that the term "dead weight" was true for a short person like me.

"Anyway you can, without jostling or bumping the body too much," was the response.

With this type of transfer, stretcher to stretcher it wasn't hard. A quick pull starting with the feet was enough to slide it over. There was blood on the green sheet below the body and I asked why.

"Autopsy," was the response. He locked the morgue door and wheeled the stretcher to the vehicle, deftly loading in one smooth motion. It looked easy enough, but I learned the hard way over time that you do need to be fit and strong to make it look that easy. The empty stretcher weighs about seventy pounds. A female should be able to lift half their weight. The stretcher alone was over half of my weight and if one added a two-hundred-pound body, that exceed my ability.

The director handed me the keys and said he would meet me at the front of the hospital, he was going to return the morgue key. Under the Funeral Directors and Establishments Act (Bill 30) if the vehicle has windows they must be blacked out. The transfer vehicle was a station wagon with darkened rear windows which meant if you were backing up you had to learn to use the side mirrors exclusively.

My personal vehicle had a stick shift and it had been over ten years since I'd driven an automatic, but I made it out of the laneway and around to the front of the hospital without incident, smiling in triumph. Even the simplest tasks such as running a reception, driving a transfer vehicle, helping load a stretcher were new to me, and it felt good to be able to complete them without letting it show I hadn't done them before.

Once we arrived at the funeral home I backed into the garage and watched as the director unloaded the stretcher and took it to the preparation room. I didn't follow him into the prep room because before I was allowed to observe in the prep I had to earn the privilege and prove to the directors that I was serious and committed to funeral service.

Over the next few weeks I paid my dues washing vehicles, vacuuming, dusting, running errands, cleaning bathrooms, etc. Housework on a grand scale but fussier, the vacuuming had to be perfect. It was like mowing a lawn, covering miles of carpet and often done several times a day. The vacuum left lines in the carpet and it was important to get the "tracks" straight. We called it mowing the suites and warned other staff members to keep off the grass. It was rather annoying to see unnecessary footprints on a freshly mowed carpet.

As I am somewhat task oriented and focused, the directors took great glee in sneaking up behind me while I was vacuuming and watching me jump and shriek in fright. More than once they startled me to the point my legs gave out, much to their merriment.

One afternoon I answered a call that caught me off guard. An elderly lady called with a donation. She explained that she and the deceased had been best friends for years. In a voice choked with tears she asked me how her friend looked. At a loss for words I responded something to the effect that she looked good and the lady, now in full sobs, hung up. From then on, I made it a point to take a few minutes to view the deceased, taking note of what they were wearing so I could be prepared to answer that question. It must be very difficult for lifelong friends or family confirmed to a nursing home or in hospital who cannot attend the service. Sometimes there's no chance to say goodbye and I knew I had to be sensitive to their need to know.

My forty-hour observation period was drawing to a close. By now, I had done just about everything except observe in the preparation room. I took matters into my own hands, went downstairs, stood at the prep room door and asked outright if I might observe. The funeral director was hesitant and I could see that, but I really did want to get an idea of what to expect. He gave his permission somewhat reluctantly, with a strong warning not to repeat what went on in the preparation room. While the procedure is generic, talking about the deceased is not acceptable outside the room (Bill 30), it would be a breach of confidentiality and could be considered misconduct.

Funeral service in Ontario in the late 1980's was governed by the Ministry of Consumer and Commercial Relations. For years, it had been under the Ministry of Health. The newer legislation ensured consumer protection for prepaid contracts and trust funds, making the Act consumer and contract oriented. The Ministry of the Environment also monitored the funeral industry. The training for a licence in Ontario is more extensive than in other provinces and the regulations were strictly enforced.

Embalming itself is no secret, authors writing exposes of the industry gave detailed and sometimes slightly macabre accounts of the embalming process.

My first observation of the embalming process was minimal and not quite what I had expected. Like the first exposure to the morgue, it was somewhat anticlimactic. The prep room looked a bit like an operating room. It was furnished with a sink, cupboards and a table that could be raised, lowered and tilted. The embalming machine looked like a piece of medical equipment and the instruments were medical. A tube ran from the machine to the body, where a tiny incision had been made. That was all I saw that night. It would be much later before I fully knew about the complexities of embalming.

Once my forty hours was complete I continued to volunteer. One of the directors asked me to blow dry and style the deceased's hair, my first time working solo in the prep room. He went off on an errand, leaving me alone in the funeral home. I quietly went to work. It was just like drying my children's hair and even though the tangles were not going to hurt I performed the task with the same gentleness and was conscious of the need for dignity.

The director came back just as I was finishing and asked if I had been alone in a prep room before. It hadn't occurred to him as he left that perhaps I might not have been. He told me later had he known, he wouldn't have left me alone. It didn't bother me, I appreciated the opportunity.

My daughter still wasn't keen on having to admit what her mother was doing for a living so I decided, with the managing director's permission, to make her face reality once and for all and put an end to the negativism. She had been to funerals. I did not hide the truth from her or protect her from the obvious. It was time for a reality check.

It started with a visit to the funeral home. I gave her the same tour I received my first day. She sat in a funeral coach. I showed her how to use the empty stretcher for transfers and let her load it into the vehicle. Making sure all the lights were on so her overactive imagination wasn't fueled I took her to the door of the empty preparation room. That part of the tour was rather anticlimactic for her.

The following day she came to work with me, carried flowers, helped wheel the casket to the suite, laid out the register book, made coffee and dusted and vacuumed. By the end of the day I could see a slight change in her demeanor and attitude. A few days later one of the directors asked if she would like to accompany him on an out-of-town transfer. His positive attitude and good humour was the turning point. No more “my mother works with dead things” – that stage passed and she didn’t wrinkle her nose when she talked about funeral service anymore.

CHAPTER TWO

I Can Handle This

One night while assisting a director in the preparation room, I offered to style the deceased's hair. Normally a hairdresser comes in but it was late and visitation was to be held the following day. It didn't look too bad when I finished but I wasn't completely satisfied.

The next afternoon. I brought in a curling iron to complete the final touches. The casket was to be closed so it probably didn't matter but I never took that attitude. The family is encouraged to spend a few minutes with the casket open prior to receiving their visitors. The funeral director had not yet arrived and as I surveyed my work I heard the front door open.

Peeking around the corner of the suite my heart skipped a beat. The family had arrived and there was no funeral director to greet them and usher them into the suite. It would be his responsibility to suggest to the family they might want to have the casket open for a few minutes, not mine.

I quickly hid the curling iron behind a couch and went down the hall to take their coats. In my haste, I forgot to lower the lid of the casket. As I walked them to the suite and informed them that if there was anything they wished to change to let us know. I have since learned not to back myself into a corner. I now ask, “is everything satisfactory” and then leave them alone to acclimatize. Secretly I hoped they would not mention the hair.

We paused at the door of the suite. One family member walked confidently to the casket and started sobbing. I had a moment of panic.

“Oh, she looks lovely,” she said. The other family member stood at the door looking apprehensive.

“It’s all right,” I said, touching her hand.

“I can’t,” she replied.

“I know it’s hard. I’ll go with you.” She gripped my arm tightly and we walked to the casket with the encouragement of the other family member. I stood with her until she released the grip she had on my arm and then I quietly retreated, leaving them to their grief.

With no experience with families and not knowing the procedure for the first visit, I wasn't sure I'd handled it correctly. The telephone rang and the funeral director on call asked how things were going. "The family is here," I said.

"What? They're an hour early!"

I assured him things seemed to be fine.

"I'll be right in." And true to his word, he arrived about ten minutes later. The family asked that the casket be left open. After visitation, I retrieved the curling iron from its hiding place in the suite.

Shortly after my experience with this family, I saw my first autopsied body. It was a coroner's case, and the autopsy was performed to determine the cause of death. The deceased was the same age as me, which added to my consternation.

My first reaction was one of shock. I'd never seen an autopsied body before. My legs started to tremble at the sight of the open body cavity. The funeral director explained everything he was doing as we went along. I didn't ask very many questions and was rather quiet. The embalming and preparation of an autopsied body can take two to three hours.

An autopsy usually involves removal of the thoracic (chest) and abdominal organs. It is usually accompanied by a cranial autopsy, that is, the brain is removed. The trunk incision may run from just below the chin to the pubic area and across the chest. The cranial incision is behind the head from ear to ear.

There are several types of autopsy incisions. The organs are placed in a plastic bag and then returned to the abdominal cavity. At first, I wondered why the organs were not incinerated at the hospital, but it's important that all body parts accompany the remains, out of respect for the deceased and for medical/legal reasons.

There are two ways to pack the viscera back into the body cavity; treat the viscera with strong embalming fluid or cut and dry pack it in embalming powder. Years ago, autopsies were performed in funeral homes, especially in outlying areas, with the funeral director serving as the pathologist's assistant.

Occasionally, a family will ask the funeral director whether or not they did the right thing consenting to an autopsy. It's never acceptable for a director to express a negative opinion at this point. Some do, however. We usually ask if the autopsy procedure was explained to them, if not, we explain it and reassure them that if the doctors requested the autopsy, there was a reason. We do our best to reassure them that restoration is not a problem if they are concerned about the appearance of the deceased.

A few days after that first experience with the autopsied body the director asked if I wanted to observe again. It had taken several days to clear the images of the first experience from my mind, and I know it will continue to be indelibly etched in my memory for the rest of my life.

This time, however, was different. I knew what to expect and was clinically interested in the process. The funeral director was very considerate. He asked me to assist him with part of the procedure and once involved, I forgot how queasy I had been. Again, I was impressed by the professionalism of the funeral director. There were no sick jokes or off-colour remarks. This was someone's parent, spouse, or sibling. I had the distinct impression that the spirit of the person on the table was around us watching.

Under the Government of Ontario Anatomy Act medical embalming is performed differently than regular embalming. It is a closed system, that is, no drainage of blood takes place. The body is injected (usually via the carotid artery) with a large amount of embalming fluid of a moderate index. The end result is a well-preserved cadaver used to train medical personnel.

Later that week we had a funeral service where there were dozens of flower arrangements. The suite was filling up and still they came, each arrangement uniquely beautiful.

Each time I took an arrangement into the suite while the family was present they inspected it carefully, as if each bouquet was being judged. The flowers appeared to mean a great deal to this family. The flowers spilled into other rooms and the funeral home looked and smelled like a flower shop. It was a major challenge for the family to agree on what three arrangements would go to the church, the decision was a political one.

It was almost impossible for the directors to work on flower placement together. One positions a bouquet only to have another move it. After having all my placements rearranged I bowed out, leaving the “war of the roses” to the senior director.

In between visitations that day, the funeral director was called to do a removal from a nursing home out of town.

It was wet and snowy, a nasty day. He asked me to bring a cremation container up from downstairs. Lifting is part of being an undertaker but it wasn't easy for me. It took about twenty minutes to wrestle the container onto a church truck (an expandable wheeled unit used to move caskets) and load it into the service car. I was soaked with perspiration and shaky from the effort. Perhaps that's why what happened next affected me the way it did. We locked the door to the garage and removed the stretcher from the car. The deceased was elderly and quite emaciated. He was not wrapped in a sheet (the funeral director explained why later). He was wearing a tattered nightshirt and diaper. He smelled. His eyes were open and his mouth gaped. As I took all this in I couldn't help but think there is no dignity in death.

We discussed the best way to move him into the cremation container. As the director and I lifted him all the director said was "gently". So as carefully and kindly as we were able to, we placed this poor old man into the box. We stood and looked at him for a few minutes. The garage was very quiet. I wished later that I had gone into the funeral home and taken one flower from the many arrangements left from the previous funeral and placed it in the box.

There was no one to mourn his passing. Once we sealed the container and scrubbed our hands the funeral director broke the silence and expressed his opinion.

"Money aside, what would you rather see, the funeral inside or this?" He sounded almost angry but I understood. No family, no instructions, just immediate disposition. If he had a family and they were unable to pay for the service, the funeral home may have provided the service at no charge. Social services will pay the basic cost.

He then went on to explain why the gentleman had not been wrapped in a sheet. The nurse at the senior's home was sullen and not very co-operative. There was no privacy and as the funeral director slid the body from the bed to the stretcher the nurse snatched the sheet away. Rather than leave the task unfinished to go down to the service car for another sheet, he simply completed the transfer with as much dignity as possible. There were other residents in the area and he did not want to upset them more than necessary. All-in-all a rather depressing situation.

Sometimes nursing home removals are awkward. Walking past the residents with a stretcher and a body bag containing one of their companions is uncomfortable. If I were in their position I'm sure I'd be wondering if I was next. Many nursing homes do not have a morgue or a quiet location to place the deceased near an outside door. Not very logical considering most of the residents will be leaving with a funeral director someday.

That incident affected me deeply. A few days later I mailed in my application to Humber College. When I first started working in funeral service as an observer, I found every minute enjoyable. After I had been observing for several months my feelings for the work expanded, I became less self-centred and intrigued, and more client centred. It was time to take the final step to begin training.

In late January, some forms arrived from Humber College. There was a five-page questionnaire containing such questions as "What do you consider the five most important facets of a funeral director?" and "When did you first decide on funeral service as a career?" There was an evaluation form to be completed by the funeral home where the observation period had taken place and an interview form.

The thought of an interview was daunting. Interviewers usually make up their minds in the first few minutes. I recalled a recent conversation with a gentleman who had come into the office to make a donation. He had asked me if I was a funeral director. "Not yet," I had replied.

"So why do you want to be one?" he asked.

I hesitated.

"You know, if they do interviews would they not ask that question?"

He was right. I didn't have a simple answer. There were a number of reasons, none of which overrode the others in terms of importance to me.

One reason was the grief process. Idealistically perhaps I believed that a funeral director's role was that of a facilitator, not a functionary in the grief process. The opportunity to stand beside someone at their deepest level of pain was a privilege.

I also liked how a funeral director spent their day. You could be extremely busy for a number of hours, then sit down and chat over coffee for an hour or two.

I found embalming interesting. Peer support was of significant interest to me. How can an ambulance attendant, police officer, funeral director view or pick up a mutilated body, deal with a tragic death and walk away unaffected? Debriefing each other should take place quickly in order to avoid burnout and attrition. "Death overload" costs in terms of training of new personnel and in the emotional and mental toll the trauma exacts on the participant and their family.

Community education was another task a funeral director could perform. Teaching the living about death and the preparation and management for a funeral was becoming part of the role of funeral service personnel.

All-in-all I could only say that I wanted to be a funeral director because of the above. I wasn't sure what answer the interviewer wanted, and with so many applications and limited positions available I had to get it right.

It took a long time to fill in the forms. The funeral director who evaluated me was very generous and I appreciated his kindness.

As it turned out, there was no interview, it had been abolished. Interviews can be subjective and as such, can violate the applicant's human rights.

The next day I mailed the forms and asked the funeral director if I could continue observing. He agreed and later that night, around 10:30 p.m. he called. He had a house call and asked if I would assist. I lived too far from the funeral home to arrive in a timely fashion so I had to decline, but asked if I could help with the preparation. He agreed and I proceeded into town.

The deceased was a young woman who left behind a husband and children. When I told the director how much I appreciated being allowed to assist him, he responded that he was glad for the company, cases like that one were hard.

Our hearts were heavy when we discussed the effect her death had on her young family.

"This could be you or me," I remarked to him and we looked at each other for a few seconds before he slowly nodded. We finished around 2:00 a.m. The visitation was the next day, and well attended. The funeral director asked if I wanted to assist at the funeral. This was to be my first opportunity to assist at a church service.

The director and I rode in the lead car. He explained how to lead a procession and what need to be done by the staff at the church. During the drive, I asked him what he wanted me to do when we arrived.

"I'm thinking about it," was his response.

We wheeled the casket to the front of the church and placed the flowers and pictures of the young mother and her family on the casket. Standing back to survey our work he gave me my assignment. At the close of the service we were to pair up, walk down the aisle where I was to step forward, remove the pictures from the casket and ask the pallbearers to accompany me out of the sanctuary. The service was simple and meaningful.

As it ended my stomach clenched but I looked straight ahead, walked to the casket, picked up the pictures and turned to the pallbearers as the staff took their place at each end of the casket.

"Gentleman, would you follow me please?" The pallbearers ignored me. Ever alert, the director stepped in.

"Gentleman, this way please," and this time they complied. I started up the aisle. Although the pallbearers had been instructed to walk in pairs I turned my head to see a straggling set of men. I had no credibility, it was like herding cats. One commented about a woman's role outside, which I wisely chose to ignore.

The next time I issued instructions at a funeral it was in a clear authoritative voice.

Because funeral directors attend so many services it would seem logical they would be bored. Perhaps some are, but each life is recognized and celebrated, making each service special.

Later that week I drove pallbearers to a cemetery service. When I climbed into the car they stopped talking. I knew of only one female funeral director in our area and it felt awkward. However, it was my job to be their chauffeur, not make small talk.

I gave them their cemetery instructions hoping they had no way of knowing it was my first cemetery service. During the committal service as a driver I stood by the car, it was the director's job to be with the family, support staff stayed back until it was time to return to the funeral home.

Working with clergy, an important part of a funeral director's job, was interesting too. Some view you as part of the team, working with you to assist the family through their grief; others can be disdainful, critical or distant.

One evening as one of the directors discussed arrangements with a family, he had to answer the phone. After he identified himself he was greeted with a cheery, “Hi, how the hell are you?”

The director maintained his composure and responded, “Oh yes, Rev. Jones. How are you?”

The minister picked up the cue and replied, “You are with a family?”

The director responded with, “Yes, that is correct,” which fueled the minister’s mischievous streak and he did his best to make the director laugh.

A few days later prior to the service I had the opportunity to meet this man. The director came down the hallway beside the chapel with the robed clergyman.

The funeral director introduced him, “Rev. Jones, I would like you to meet Jan Richardson. Jan – this is Rev. Jones.”

I smiled sweetly, extended my hand. “Rev. Jones, it’s nice to meet you. How the hell are you?” The ensuing burst of laughter showed his good humour.

In early February a letter arrived from Humber College. A general information session and testing was being held at the end of the month. I called the college and asked if they had a list of funeral homes in the Toronto area that accepted first year students as employees. The secretary gave me names of funeral homes and I arranged for job interviews the week of the tests.

I enjoyed all aspects of funeral service but I was hoping for an opportunity to work with a transfer service, also known as a funeral directors service, a company that supports funeral homes with removals and transfers, vehicles, embalming, licenced and unlicensed staff for services, and sometimes repatriation. They also did on call work for coroner's removals.

When I called, they offered to let me follow one of their employees for a day. I was told the pace was hectic, busy twenty-four hours a day. I couldn't wait.

The day before the Humber information session and testing I arrived at the transfer service. We went to and from hospitals to funeral homes and did a few house calls.

As we were leaving one of the many hospitals in the Toronto area there was a solid clunk under our feet and the car stopped moving. The transmission broke. The cars were radio equipped and the director radioed base for assistance.

Our first priority was to push the car off the street. A small knot of bystanders watched. I asked one of the men standing on the sidewalk if he would please give us a hand pushing our service car to the curb. He just looked at me.

Living in a small town, if your vehicle breaks down usually the first person who comes along stops to assist. I shrugged and started pushing, which goaded some of the men into action and it was moved to the curb.

I went foraging for coffee and donuts which we shared with our helpers. There was no way you could leave the car and take a bus back to the office if there was a body on board.

It took the tow truck about an hour and a half to arrive, apparently normal in the big city. It gave me a chance to quiz the director about his career and what his job was like. When the tow truck driver arrived, he scowled and asked if we had a body in the car. Normally that question could not be answered but the tow truck driver was one of the "need to know" personnel. The director replied in the affirmative and the tow truck driver went to radio his dispatcher, making in clear in no uncertain terms that he would not touch our vehicle and made it even clearer he was not doing the call.

The director intercepted him. We were a block and a half from the funeral home and we had to get there. Obviously, it was up to the tow truck driver to do his job so we could do ours. The director tried to reason with him. It was difficult to tell what the tow truck driver was thinking.

With a sigh, he proceeded to jack up the front of the car, grumbling that he shouldn't have to tow dead bodies. There was a distinct thump as the stretcher hit the back door. That would have been horrible if the back door had flown open and the deceased had been dumped onto the street!

We delivered the deceased without incident to the funeral home and took a cab back to base. It had been an amazing day and I hated to see it end. To my delight, I was asked if I wanted to return for another observation day after my day at the college.

The following morning was cold and snowy. Would-be students stood outside the lecture hall at Humber quiet and sober. The Pharmacy,

Ambulance and Emergency Care applicants were testing with the Funeral Service applicants. I sat and people watched. It was easy to spot some of the Funeral Service applicants, black coat, funeral suit, the benign look.

The testing consisted of reading comprehension and vocabulary. Not too bad. The next two tests were a complete surprise. We were given a science test that covered material in the Ontario Advanced Credit biology course that I had sweated through seven months before and then promptly put behind me once the credit was earned. By the completion of that test I was feeling defeated. I knew one answer of out the sixty was correct, the rest were uneducated guesses. The final test was an essay test. We were given an hour and a half to complete it.

We then adjourned to a classroom where Professor John Finn gave information about the program. John was tall with a deep, voice. I was quite intimidated by him. He commanded immediate respect.

We were told that a funeral director usually spends ten percent of his/her time in the preparation room. Ninety percent of our time was spent with the living. He suggested that with the heavy course load that working part-time would not be advisable. However, for those who had no choice but to work, a list was passed around for signatures for interviews with local funeral homes.

The list was long by the time it reached me. I was glad I had started my search early, it was likely that the jobs would go to younger, stronger students. A part-time job would have been ideal during the school year, but knowing I still had to send money home to my family and pay my rent and expenses in Toronto, I would have to work full time hours and attend school full time.

I left the college with a pounding headache coupled with a sense of foreboding. Many of the applicants had post-secondary education at a university level.

Before returning home I still had one more day at the transfer service I had applied to. We had a body to deliver to Humber College. My partner/mentor did his best to orient me to the streets around Humber, but it was confusing. I was lost.

Driving around campus to somewhere at the rear he backed the service car down a ramp and rang the bell. After a bit of a wait he told me to stay there while he went around the building. I stood shivering at the back door of the service car. Suddenly the garage door opened and there stool Professor Finn. We looked at each other and all I could think was that he looked more intimidating than ever.

A few seconds passed before I realized that obviously I had to complete the transfer without my partner and to get started. I struggled and wrestled with the stretcher. Professor Finn stood by passively and watched. Finally, the stretcher was free and I tugged it into the garage. My partner came through the lab door in front of me as John closed the garage door.

"You are going to have to do better than that if you're going to be a funeral director," John said dryly. He proceeded into the lab. My partner caught my eye. My cheeks burned. John was ahead of us in the lab waiting and watched as we transferred the body. I glanced around the lab quickly.

There were three preparation tables. The counters and sinks gleamed. I wondered if I would ever work in it. I listened to the two men's small talk keeping my head down, still smarting from the remark. Closing the stretcher cover, I then pushed it to the transfer vehicle, waited for the garage door to open and shoved the 70 lb stretcher into the service car with a bit more finesse then when I had removed it. Again, John stood tall and silent watching. I felt clumsy and awkward under his scrutiny.

"How did you find the testing?" John asked suddenly, breaking the silence. He startled me with his question. I could feel my heart thumping. My partner discreetly backed away. John couldn't know who I was, there were dozens of people in the information session. I reassured myself that at least he couldn't know my name. The last thing I wanted to do was to stick out. I planned to keep a low profile in the event I was accepted into the Funeral Service program.

I swallowed hard. "To be honest, I found the science test difficult."

How did you do on the Nelson-Denny?" John asked.

"I didn't finish it. I managed to complete ninety seven out of the one hundred vocabulary questions, but I ran out of time.

"You did well," John said kindly. "Most applicants complete about fifty percent. The Nelson-Denny is an important test." John looked at me intently and again I had the feeling I was under evaluation.

As we drove away, I voiced my feelings to my partner. “He just stood there and watched and didn’t even try to help. I made a complete fool of myself,” I sputtered. My partner burst out laughing. I failed to see the humour.

“Get used to it,” he said. “And you will have to do better than that if you plan on being a funeral director. You’ll learn to lift better after a few weeks on the job here.” His tone was almost ominous. “That is, if you last.” He looked at me sideways. “If you do get into Humber you’ll find that John will be one of your favourite people.”

I didn’t reply, I just didn’t believe him. I also failed to grasp what he said about lasting on the job, it was back at base I learned I’d been hired by the transfer service, he’d given me a good evaluation.

Many months later I reminded John of our first encounter.

“I was just testing you,” John chuckled.

I laughed too. He had known that day that I had been accepted into Humber.

While scouting for positions in Toronto I met a second-year student who was completing an apprenticeship. This person was disillusioned and bitter. She stated that her goal was to complete the program and get her licence. Having the licence was a means to an end so she would have something to fall back on in the future. This individual had many quarrels with funeral service as a career, not the least of which were long hours and poor pay.

About a week after my return from Toronto a letter arrived from one of the funeral homes I had visited. To my surprise, I was offered a position for the summer. This funeral home offered some unique opportunities because it was located in an ethnic community.

I accepted the position with one reservation, the thought of leaving my family several months early wasn't pleasant, but I had no choice. In the few months before the acceptance letters for college came, I was determined to get as much experience as I could. Until then I continued to work part-time at the funeral home where I had first observed.

Back in my home town on a rainy, muddy day, the coach driver, limo driver, and I were asked to go to the cemetery for a committal. We were to place the casket on the grave and wait for the family and funeral director to arrive. The casket was a little heavier than we had anticipated. We struggled through the mud to the grave and tried to place the casket on the straps. It caught on the straps and in the ensuring off-balance struggle to lift it we slipped in the mud. The front of the casket tipped dangerously downwards.

Fortunately, the limo driver at the back kept it from slipping into the grave. Had that happened, we would have had to get the cemetery staff with a lift to remove it, and with the family on the way that would have been a dreadful situation. In hindsight, three people on a casket are three too few, it requires strength, six people and balance.

The second time I drove a funeral coach we had a church funeral and committal. It was a Catholic service and my first funeral mass. When I placed the church truck inside the door I got caught up in the crowd of pallbearers and mourners coming in.

The funeral director quietly told me to take the pallbearers and seat them in the pews on the left. I led them up the aisle and seated them on the right. One of the other directors came up behind me and whispered, “Wrong side!” This old-school director did not approve of women in funeral service and took every opportunity to reinforce his belief when we were out of the public eye.

One of the other directors motioned me to the front and said quietly, "I hope you remember how to genuflect." Earlier that day I had practiced genuflecting at home in front of the mirror, landing on my rear-end in gales of laughter, it wasn't easy to do in high heels with nothing to hold on to. In hindsight, I should have made a point of visiting various denominations and faith services in my area to prepare me for the differences so I could appear more respectful and dignified.

Details are important; understanding different faiths, denominations and religions mattered. My continued exposure to funeral service only strengthened my resolve. I wanted to be a funeral director more than ever. The road ahead was long indeed.

CHAPTER THREE

More Reality

Occasionally a body is misplaced. One evening on a hospital transfer, the security guard and I proceeded to the morgue. Hospital protocols varied, sometimes we went to the morgue alone, in that hospital the security guard unlocked the morgue door.

He opened the door and walked in. "There's no one here," he said with obvious surprise.

"I have the release, we got the call hours ago," I replied as I walked into the freezer. It wasn't a big area, there was room for four stretchers side by side. We looked at each other with puzzled expressions and for some reason, we both bent down and looked underneath the stretchers. If there had been someone under the stretchers we would have seen them from the door, so as we straightened up we both laughed.

The security guard called admitting and I called the funeral home to tell them that the body was misplaced and it could be awhile. Eventually the deceased was tracked down somewhere in the hospital. The guard and I had a good visit while we waited. He helped me load the body onto the stretcher and into the car. I rather enjoyed chatting with him.

Coroner's calls required emotional and physical strength. In the larger cities the transfer services do the coroner's work, in the rest of the province funeral home staff will respond to coroner's calls. These are usually trauma cases, homicides, accidents or sudden home deaths.

With trauma or homicide cases the scene may be hampered by snow, terrain, distance. The removal person may be required to search for pieces of the remains. It is not a position for the faint hearted. Police officers are usually invaluable in situations where a removal is difficult. More than once I relied on their strength to assist me down a flight of stairs or up a slippery embankment. The safety of the removal team is their priority.

Ideally the removal should be performed with the least possible fuss and hopefully with some dignity. Climbing down a rock cut in a director's uniform and panty hose looks a little out of place, but a black jacket, white shirt, grey or black bow and black and grey stripped skirt is the uniform we wear.

The funeral home I was working at hired a young man as an assistant. He was delightful and we worked well together. He and I were sent to a coroner's call out of town. Upon arrival, we noticed five policemen standing outside the building.

As I exited the vehicle one of the officer's remarked, "Oh great, they sent a woman." Statements like that seldom rolled off my back. They annoyed me, but I kept my feelings to myself. My partner and I exchanged glances, he knew me well enough to know that wasn't something I would take kindly to. In all fairness to the officers, they had been at the scene for a long time; it took us about an hour to respond because of the distance. I was in charge of the transfer as the more experienced individual so I stood as tall as I could at sixty inches and proceeded to enter the building.

My partner, upon entering, immediately did an about face and headed for the bushes, where he lost his lunch. I thought I would be right behind him, the smell was horrific. I desperately fought to keep myself from upchucking. When I was in

Toronto for testing, I was told by the removal service that when you encounter a situation like that to stay there. Going in and out only makes it worse.

With watery eyes and increasing nausea I studied the scene. The deceased was hanging from the ceiling, badly decomposed. It was not going to be an easy transfer. I went to the vehicle; my poor partner was useless – he was retching just thinking about the call.

I gathered the supplies, a body bag, extra sheet and the stretcher. Up to that point I had ignored the officer who made the comment about me being a woman and asked the general group if anyone had the death certificate. His senior officer handed it over and I placed it in the van.

This time three officers followed me in, including the one who didn't think a woman could/should do the job. Even a short trip to the van meant my nose and stomach had to start all over again.

I heard two of the officers start to retch and watched them head for the bushes, including the one who had made the comment. The senior officer and I were the only ones left. He shrugged, headed to the body and while I lifted it up he cut it down. Flies and maggots are unpleasant and the body was slippery, but you do your best to get past it and try to preserve some dignity for the deceased.

Once we had the deceased on the floor, I could see the officer was struggling with the smell. I suggested he go outside for some air and I would finish up. He disappeared out the door as I thanked him for his help. There was no way anyone could have done the job alone.

Truthfully though, I wasn't sure I could get the job done. I was getting desperate. The bushes were calling me. But the officer's remark about women won out and, although it took a bit longer than I would have liked, no one could see me fighting back the nausea since I was alone.

Exiting with the stretcher it was a quiet group that watched me. Fresh air had never smelled sweeter. My partner waited at the vehicle and he opened the van door so I could load the body. I caught his eye and headed for the driver's seat.

I turned to thank the senior officer for his assistance, changed my mind and climbed into the passenger side of the van and said to my partner through gritted teeth, "Get the heck out of here now!" I cranked down the window once we were more or less out of sight and earshot of the police and sucked as much air into my lungs as I could between retching.

I reassured my remorseful partner that the only reason I didn't get sick like everyone else was because of the remark made by the officer. Pride goes before a fall I told him, but this time I was too angry and that was the only reason I narrowly escaped joining them at the bushes.

It's inappropriate to discuss the details of a call with anyone other than your colleagues. After a gruesome removal, it's difficult to wind down. Most of the directors I have talked to remember the first time they saw an autopsied body or their first accident.

One of the senior directors recalled an accident where three victims were taken to the funeral home for autopsy, something that was done in rural areas when he first started. He, the police and the coroner worked through the night. At some point in the middle of the night one of them call his wife, got her out of bed and requested coffee and sandwiches for the crew. They stopped for a lunch break and continued with their task. He could still recall the details.

He also related how much his job had changed. Visitations were held in homes. Salaries were low and the hours long. Directors also doubled as ambulance attendants, the funeral homes at that time ran the ambulance service. He recalled delivering a baby that couldn't wait until the mother got to the hospital, then later that day preparing a body. He summed it up succinctly – hatched and dispatched.

Funeral homes were also staffed twenty-four hours a day before pagers. He used to be responsible for wheeling the caskets to the front door of the funeral home after visitation. In the event of a fire it was his responsibility to push the casket out onto the street. He recalled that the funeral home was on a hill and it seemed foolish. He remembered how hard it was to prepare the body of a friend or relative. The fact that he stayed in his chosen career all his life was a testament to his dedication to families in need.

Up to this point my involvement consisted of reception, removals, funerals and preparation room assisting. I did recognize acquaintances among the visitors, we might have gone to school together, but the families I encountered were strangers to me.

Early one morning I arrived at the funeral home with muffins. The coffee was on but the director was nowhere to be found. After scouting the obvious places, I headed for the preparation room. My greeting stopped mid-sentence I stood frozen on the spot. The deceased was a friend.

Tears immediately blinded my eyes and I instinctively reached out to touch the body. At a loss for words I turned and left. Pouring myself a coffee I sat alone and cried. Sooner or later it was bound to happen. In the larger funeral homes directors did not have to get involved with arrangements for their family or friends, their colleagues would do the work; although I came to understand that most did, the personal involvement was an act of love when it was family or a friend.

One final requirement for Humber remained, we were to complete an additional forty hours in a different funeral home. For my next observation period, I picked a funeral home in the country. It was a considerable drive from home but I had called the funeral director at the recommendation of a friend. He had a good reputation and was well-respected.

Leaving at sunrise I drove north, around lakes, through wooded areas and fields. I arrived at the funeral home about two hours later. The size of this funeral home surprised me, it was much bigger than I anticipated and bigger than the city funeral home. The doors were locked so I stood in the doorway and surveyed the village.

Small, quiet, quaint – my thoughts were interrupted by a cheery, “Oh there’s someone here.”

I introduced myself to a tall and very pleasant gentleman. “The bank manager called me to let me know a stranger was standing outside,” he said. “We look out for each other in small towns.” His house was beside his funeral home.

As we entered I was impressed by the modern and beautiful décor. Over coffee we chatted about our families and background. Each day he had a call I looked forward to returning.

The funeral home averaged one call per week. I expected visitation to be quiet. It was completely the opposite. There would be a steady stream of people, all who seemed to know each other. There was an abundance of flowers and donations. It wasn't a wake, it was a social event. The funeral home was almost too small to accommodate everyone. People greeted the funeral director like an old friend and he knew most of them by name.

The chapel was full the day of the funeral. This director had his own coach and cars. I stayed behind to clean up so when the drivers and director returned from the cemetery we had time to sit down for coffee.

I learned a great deal about funeral service from this man and his father, a semi-retired funeral director. Like most of the funeral directors I had met up to this point, he had a wonderful sense of humour.

Over the next weeks, I was to spend many happy hours there. I met his wife and family and got to know some of the people in the village. Every time I went north he made sure I was fed and he would put gas in my car. Since I was there to observe and was getting what I wanted out of the experience, I couldn't help but feel he was spoiling me. His staff were all great fun and we found all sorts of things to laugh about.

Every detail relating to the preparation of the suite, the family's first visit, the funeral and committal got his undivided attention. After the services, he looked drained and he was because he knew so many of the families. It took a lot out of him.

One afternoon when his funeral home received a death call, I offered to go to the hospital and do the removal. It took several hours because of the distance and it was dark when I returned. The garage was pitch black and I could not find the light switch. His cat, Ace, rubbed up against me in the dark.

"Darn it Ace," I grumbled. "I haven't got a clue where to find the light switch." Cracking my shin on a sharp edge I yelped. Ace rubbed up against me again and emitted a series of short, chirpy meows. I followed the sounds to the elusive light switch. I could hear laughter inside. The funeral director had heard the ruckus and was coming to the rescue. But it was Ace that showed me where to go.

Several months later, while working for the removal service in Toronto a young couple who did the out-of-town trips for their local funeral home related the following story.

They were taking a body to a small village in the middle of nowhere. It was dark and there were no street lights and no moon. The young woman didn't want to have anything to do with the bodies, she just went along to keep her husband company on long trips. Consequently, if a body was to be moved she waited in the car.

Her husband left the back door to the van open. Suddenly, she heard a distinct thump and the unmistakable rustle of something moving toward her. She froze, too frightened to move. A head poked through the curtain behind her and gave a chirpy meow. She found her voice and screamed. The rest of us in the office laughed as she related the story.

"So you met my buddy Ace," I said. They all looked at me. "Nice cat. Knows his way around the funeral home." Once she had recovered her equilibrium that night she and Ace got acquainted. That's one transfer she won't quickly forget.

By the end of April, I had completed Biology, my two forty-hour observations periods, Nursing Communications, Anatomy and Sociology. I'd been to Humber for testing, secured a job in Toronto and had only to wait for notification of acceptance into the program. The time dragged.

I tried not to think about school. I had no contingency plan should I not get into Humber. I was scheduled to start my job in Toronto in May. If I didn't get in, there'd be no job.

The day the acceptances were to be released I received a call from a friend wanting to know if I had heard anything yet. Her son had received a phone call from Humber College that morning accepting him into the program he applied to.

I called the College only to learn that the computers were down and to try again tomorrow. The next day I was told that the Funeral Service Department was still deciding on applicants and I should hear in a few weeks. I didn't have a few weeks.

I called my new employer in Toronto and explained the situation. He said he would call the college and see if they would tell him because he needed me to start right away. If I didn't make it he had to find a new employee.

The phone rang about twenty minutes later. "You made it," he said.

I thanked him and hung up. I experienced no emotions at that moment. It was a day or two later when the full impact of leaving my husband and children for a year and a half hit me.

I sat the kids down and made them promise to call at any time if they needed me. And I made my husband promise to come up as often as possible. My weekends were committed since I was working full time.

A few days later I moved to Toronto with mixed feelings. I was a little frightened. It was a large multicultural city and I didn't know my way around.

There wasn't much time to stress though, I spent my first three days at the transfer service. The pace was hectic, seldom was a shift less than twelve hours, many times it was longer. I learned to navigate the big city using maps, going from hospital to funeral home to deliver bodies.

It was a bit different because of the size of the funeral homes and the transfer service protocol – I was to transfer the body to the prep table, removed the plastic covering or body bag, positioned the head and hands, ensure that the eyes and mouth were closed and then apply moisturizing cream to the face and hands. The deceased was then covered with a clean sheet and the medical certificate pinned to the sheet. If there was a hospital ID bracelet it was left on the body.

If I did a house call then we would travel in separate vehicles, remove the deceased, and one of us would go to the funeral home, the other person on the next call. The cars had to be gassed and the supplied checked and restocked when we were able to get back to base.

Coroner's calls were the most exciting learning experience. The coroner's office in Toronto looked like a movie set with rows of metal drawers. It was open twenty-four hours a day. It was jokingly called "Club Med for the Dead". The top row of drawers were the penthouse suites.

Back at base I witnessed my first case of tissue gas. Tissue gas is caused by a bacteria, Clostridium perfringens, a gram positive anaerobic bacteria that is well known for causing gas gangrene. In a dead body it cannot be stopped and it spreads quickly.

Embalming may slow the progression if it is caught early. It's a like a red alert in a funeral home; instruments must be sterilized carefully and the prep room disinfected thoroughly or it can spread to other bodies. Usually the body is wrapped in plastic, the casket closed and the family informed about the problem.

I saw more bodies in a state of decomposition in those three days then I had up to date. Sometimes it was because the person has been dead for several days before being found. The slang term for such a body is “hummer”.

Since a decomposing body emits a gassy odour it can take a day or two to get the smell out of your system. It gets into your hair and clothing. Sometime you have olfactory déjà vu and smell the odor days later. One of the employees at the transfer service was nicknamed Hummer. He had a habit of getting the bad calls.

My first hummer call was a doozy. The coroner’s office told us to bring gloves and a pouch. The wagons are routinely stocked with such items so the coded wording was clear – the body was badly decomposed. Hummer and I teamed up, he left his vehicle a couple of blocks away. I drove in. About six houses down from the address Hummer and I knew we were in for a rough time.

The crowd that had gathered to watch were standing several houses down. There were four squad cars and a fire truck. Large blowers from the fire department were set up to disperse the odor. The day was hot and humid and the scent in the air was obvious. I immediately shut down the air conditioner in my vehicle to stop the air circulation.

"Oh, my God," said Hummer. The firemen and policemen were entering and exiting the house in respirators. A police officer approached the car.

"We've got a good one," he said. "The last time anyone saw him was five weeks ago." Hummer and I exchanged glances.

"I'm going to see if we can use the respirators," Hummer said and he left to speak to the firemen. Since everyone on site wore tanks I had no desire to go into the scene without one. The firemen were happy to oblige. A very cute fireman assisted me with the respirator.

The unit was heavy but the shoulder straps were well padded. I had never equated funeral service with such measures, naively thinking before I decided to go into funeral service that it was all about peace and quiet in a pristine funeral home.

As Hummer and I entered the home, the mess that greeted us was unlike anything I'd seen before. It was my first experience with a hoarder's environment; it was not to be my last.

We kicked debris out of our way to clear space for the stretcher. The body was difficult to see in the mess. The floor around the deceased was greasy and slippery and I wished I had rubber boots.

One of the police officers told me to stand back. I prepared the pouch while they placed a sheet over the body and carefully lifted it. Surprisingly there were no maggots and the limbs remained intact. Even through the plastic body bag the odour was intense. Hummer loaded the stretcher into my vehicle. The same good looking fireman removed my respirator and I could feel my cheeks grow warm with girlish embarrassment. I was surprised that the police officer stepped in to help, I wasn't used to seeing them take such an active role other than the time I had done the removal with the hanging victim with the police sergeant.

Once the stretcher was in the car I noticed my partner and some of the firemen and police disappear in the back yard. When he didn't come back right away I went to check things out.

There they were all smoking cigarettes, a habit I quickly developed. It helped clear some of the gaseous odor from my lungs. A neighbour approached with some ice water which we gratefully accepted in the ninety-degree heat. Since I was driving back to the Coroner's office it also meant I would have something on my stomach if I threw up.

Hummer turned to the police officer who had assisted us. “I take it my partner won’t get a ticket if she speeds?” he asked. The officer snorted.

“Lady,” he said, “I would be the last one to give you a ticket.” My smile was a little weak. The Coroner’s Office was about an hour’s drive from the scene. I should have asked for an escort.

I drove my partner back to his vehicle and started off again. It didn’t take too long to realize that there had to be a better way to get through the maze of traffic. Turning on my emergency flashers, I sped up, driving with one hand. The other hand was holding my jacket over my mouth and nose. My eyes were stinging and watering from the intense odor. I had a map on the seat beside me, but it was hard to read. I heard a horn and my partner pulled up in the lane beside me.

“Follow me!” he yelled. I kept on his tail as he led me through the streets. He told me later that at the stop lights he could smell the body even though he was in a separate vehicle ahead of me.

The ordeal was almost over, when a few blocks from the Coroner’s Office I encountered a road block. Crowds lined the streets. Ahead I could see gold-helmeted motorcycle officers leading a procession of limousines. A visiting ruler from another country was riding with the Premier, smiling and waving at the throngs of well-wishers. Meanwhile, people were starting to back away from my vehicle. The look of disgust on their faces said it all. Since I still had my face covered with my jacket I could hide my chuckle. How ridiculous it seemed, the most important person in the city passing by and my vehicle held the smelliest.

While it gave me pause that the poor man died alone, it was with considerable relief that I was able to transfer him to the low temperature (decomposition room) at the Coroner's Office a few minutes later.

Back at base supper was waiting. There was a time when eating after a removal similar to that one would have been impossible for me. Another call came in as we were finishing.

This time, the deceased was on the top floor of a building in a small room with no ventilation. He'd been dead about seven hours. Even in that short period of time his extremities were turning black. Summer in the removal business was not pleasant.

During that three-day period working at the transfer service I put in forty hours, picked up two suicides, one homicide, did a lot of hospital, nursing home transfers, house calls and an out of town trip. I saw a young woman who had been shot and learned about cadaveric spasm, her face was rigid with horror. It is not a common phenomenon. It did shake me up a bit.

I had the opportunity to watch some restorative work on a gunshot victim. The skull was pieced together and a bridge string was built over the open wound on the forehead. Melted wax was dripped in the opening.

The end result was quite surprising, the individual looked as if nothing had happened. It took the director about three hours to do the restoration. The deceased was to be returned to his family in another province. It requires an artist's touch and skill to restore a victim of an accident such as this one.

By day three I was getting tired. Toward the end of my shift I was given a run several hours out of Toronto. I located the hospital, removed the body and drove back. It was 1:00 a.m. before I reached the outskirts of Toronto.

I radioed the agency on the off chance that someone on night shift was up. Using the CB was new to me but I was aware that the airways were monitored by the Canadian Radio-television and Telecommunication Commission and it would be inappropriate to say something like, “I have a large body on board.” It had to be a benign, non-specific statement such as, “Large package, is someone at base to assist?” There was no reply and I felt a little lost. My day had started over fifteen hours earlier and I was exhausted.

Pulling into base I was surprised to see one of the funeral directors who lived in the apartment in the building standing on the loading dock. He opened the door to the wagon and proceeded to tell me that I had put the body on the stretcher backwards and in the event of a rear end accident with the transfer vehicle, the body would sustain less damage if it had been done correctly. Never mind that it could end up in the front seat with me.

I apologized and asked if I had wakened him when I radioed in

“No, the phones did. I just happened to hear you on the radio.”

"You could have gone back to bed and no one would have known," I said. "Thanks for your help, I really appreciate it."

He growled something back and I smiled.

He would repeat this scenario several times over my time there and he became one of my favourite supervisors. With the hours he worked, sleep was a precious commodity.

Four days after my arrival in Toronto I started my new job at the funeral home. I had yet to mentally and emotionally process all of the events over the past few days at the transfer service. I'd seen more in that three days than most directors would see in a year.

I was struck by the depravity and cruelty and evil of murder and saddened by the loneliness of death for the people who died alone. The sudden ending of a young person's life in an accident, the child who died of cancer, all sat in my memory.

Over time I would process each one, grieving for their family even though I did not know them. The "professional" front I presented on the job wasn't the total me. I felt empathy for each person I encountered.

My first day at the new funeral home started with introductions to the staff and a tour of the very large facility. I got lost a few times. There were three floors and a number of suites.

The director who was training me was a young man who graduated ten years before and had worked at that funeral home since then. He'd made arrangements for an appointment with a tailor for my funeral suit fitting. That was a new experience. Never in my life had I been fitted for a suit, not to mention the cost of such suit. I would have had to work seventy hours just to pay for it, but the funeral home paid for everything.

After a tour, fitting and coffee break he asked me to assist in the prep room. As a first year student, I was at the bottom of the pecking order and had expected to do most of the lesser tasks. He believed students should be involved in every aspect of funeral service. He was a natural teacher, and explained every detail. I was sent on a coach run at another funeral home, in a large city that was a common practice, to lend or rent out funeral vehicles.

My biggest fear was getting lost. My boss drew a map and reviewed the duties of a coach driver. Usually the coach driver places the church truck inside the door of the church and pushes the casket into and out of the church behind the minister/priest or officiate. The driver should stay with the coach as long as the casket is inside the vehicle.

As I gained more confidence over the ensuing weeks I also gave the pallbearers their instructions. It is not always a simple matter to co-ordinate six people. Occasionally one or two of them have a better idea on how to remove the casket from the coach, or go up the steps, or when to do what they think should be done.

Removing a casket from the coach requires six co-ordinated people, it's often very heavy and it was my job to position myself at the end to steady the casket. It wasn't unusual for a pallbearer to tell me they could manage without me, the "it's OK ma'am, we can do this" when I would take the front end of the casket as it was coming out of the coach became commonplace. I would smile and thank them, they were being gentlemen, but it was my job to ensure the safety of the pallbearers and the deceased. One stumble or slip from a pallbearer could result in a dropped casket. It happens.

At the cemetery, the coach driver and the limo drivers placed the flowers. Sometimes the limo and coach drivers do parking lot duty at the church or funeral home prior to the procession. As the procession is preparing to leave, they check to ensure the cars lights are on and each vehicle has a flag, (plastic signs that say funeral which are placed on the hood of each car in the procession). The coach driver is dismissed immediately after the committal and leaves before the family and mourners.

My boss and I were to become good friends. He was a compassionate, caring funeral director who did all he could for the families he served. He talked about his job and how it affected him. He had a healthy balance in his life, his time off was spent resting, on hobbies and friends.

He was funny and could make me laugh to the point of tears. He understood that I was experiencing culture shock and missing my family. A visiting casket salesman overhead all the merriment and laughter and asked the owner if that was someone crying.

"No, that's just my new employee. She's laying an egg." I loved my job, when there were no visitations it was fun. When there was a family or visitation, it was enlightening and meaningful.

Sometimes though, fatigue could affect our job performance. Funerals involve a series of tasks and details, over one hundred for a traditional funeral. With several funerals, it would be one of those days when we were overtired and overworked and giggly.

I had flagged the meters in front of the church earlier with “Funeral – NO PARKING” signs. Nonetheless, as the procession pulled up to the church, someone was sitting in their car where the coach was to go. My boss was in the lead car and he waved his hand out of the window. I pulled up behind him. He waved again. Thinking it was my cue, I pulled out in front of the two cars and trapped the trespasser. However, that was not what he wanted.

As we exited our vehicles he informed me that the coach never breaks procession. First mistake.

Going into the church I took my place at the head of the casket and proceeded up the aisle to the pall. Since the service was in Portuguese I had no idea what was being said. When the priest paused, I stepped forward, prepared to move up the aisle. I was splashed with holy water and I quickly sidestepped toward the pew. I had moved too soon. My boss gave me a look and turned toward the front of the church, refusing to look at me. Two mistakes and the funeral service hadn't even started.

I could see his shoulder's convulsing and I could hear tiny snorts of suppressed laughter. The priest carried on and when he nodded at us to proceed up the aisle, we split left and right. My boss bowed, I genuflected. The limo driver beside me bowed. We turned and exited the church, that service was to be an hour and we didn't need to stay. Once outside the two of us collapsed with laughter. The limo driver was not too impressed with our nonsense.

We went to a doughnut shop where the limo driver proceeded to inform me that I should always follow the director's lead and bow if he bowed. I had been under the impression that one genuflected in a catholic church, clearly I was wrong – in that church you bowed. I should have glanced over at him and watched to see what he was going to do.

Over doughnuts and coffee the subject of funerals became the topic of choice. I mentioned that I wanted to be buried in my stripes in a line of casket that had birds in flight as a motif.

My boss described the casket he wanted to be buried in. The limo driver had enough.

"What is with you two?" he said crossly.

My boss and I just laughed. The limo driver was right but we were too far gone to get a grip.

As we walked back to the church my boss remembered that a late arrival had pulled up across the street and asked for a funeral sign for the drive to the cemetery. He crossed the road, flagged the car and came back. Three men came out of a restaurant across the street waving their arms and shouting at us. Their message was not in English but it was clear, he had flagged the wrong car.

He headed back across the road to retrieve the flag while I collapsed on the bumper of the coach in laughter.

Pulling ourselves together, things proceeded uneventfully until we reached the cemetery. He handed me the keys to the lead car and asked the limo driver to assist me with the flowers. After the committal, I was dismissed and I drove off.

The cemetery gate was about two miles away and I drove slowly and respectfully. The funeral home plates were in the window of the coach and there were other committals in the cemetery. It was important not to draw negative attention, one doesn't smoke or listen to the radio even with an empty vehicle.

The front gate was closed. A cemetery worker informed me that I would have to take an alternate route out.

"There's a procession coming out," I said "I will try to steer them the other way." I wheeled the coach around only to see our limo coming toward me. I rolled down the window and told him the front gate was blocked. By this time, the limo driver had no respect for me and he fixed me with an icy stare.

"You have his keys," he said curtly, as if to say "your career in funeral service is over". I had pocketed the keys for the lead car after opening the trunk to retrieve the flowers. I sped up, ignoring the "Please drive slowly" signs.

A lone Cadillac sat on the road. My boss was standing beside and as I approached he pretended to shoot me. The priest had to ride back with the mourners, he had another service and needed to get back to his church. Of course we had a good laugh. I also remembered everything I did wrong that day and learned from it, recognizing how important it is not to make a bad impression. It's very hard when tired not to get the giggles.

Laughter in a funeral home seems like a misnomer, but it is not unusual to see a family laughing during a service or at a visitation. Laughter and grief are closely related. Most of the directors I knew were very funny people. I felt at home with funeral service personnel, it was as if I'd found my species.

One morning as I came off the subway on my way to work, a man on a bicycle took a nasty fall in front of me, smashing his head on the pavement. He was bleeding from a cut on his head and was semiconscious. I asked a passerby to call an ambulance. Within four minutes of my request a policeman arrived. He was very gentle with the injured man. Kneeling beside me on the pavement he asked my name and place of employment.

I quietly and discreetly replied. "The funeral home around the corner," and I gave the name of the transfer service I worked at on my days off. He chuckled.

"So are your clients usually this lively?" he asked. Once I was free to continue on my way to work I turned the wrong corner and got temporarily lost. These things keep one humble.

Work at the transfer service filled my off hours. There was a large staff; some were students like me interested in expanding their experience.

One evening the owner drove me home after my shift. It was late at night and normally I relied on buses and subways. To my embarrassment I didn't know where I lived, the route wasn't the same. He had to radio in for directions.

A great deal of good natured bantering took place there. Many days a running gag would develop at the office and the radio messages were quite entertaining. If someone went out to pick up lunch, chicken for example, they would clear the address as follows"

"…to VOC… clearing Main Street with dead chicken" It was OK to said dead chicken, it was not OK to say dead body.

If Adam was clearing a scene they would state, "Clearing hospital en route to CO's".

Harris: "You're paranoid Adam. That's the second time you radioed in. Why are you so paranoid?"

Adam: "Harris, I have an idea. There is a bus leaving for Hooterville. Why don't you get under it?"

I cut in. "Hooterville? I'll go! I want to go home. This isn't Kansas anymore."

Adam: Jan, I'm surprised at you. You know perfectly well you'll be working until nine tonight. You simply must get your priorities straight."

Downpour.

Marshall: "Oh my God, it's pouring. You should see this guy on University Street. There were two huge puddles which, of course, I missed but the next car got him. He's drenched."

Harris: "You are such a gentleman."

Me: "Hey you guys. Look at the rainbow in the East. It's beautiful."

Marshall: "Um, you're not in Kansas anymore."

Harris: (singing) ♫ "Somewhere over the rainbow…"

Jones: "What did you do with the money?"

Harris: (puzzled) "What money?"

Jones: "The money your mother gave you for singing lessons. Don't give up your day job."

Silence for several minutes.

Harris: "I'm not paranoid."

Silence for twenty minutes.

Adam: "Look at the beautiful rainbow in the east."

Me: "Auntie Em, Auntie Em! I just heard the wicked witch of the West!"

Harris: "No, she's off today. Don't mind him – he's paranoid. I've been trying to talk him into seeing a psychiatrist. He won't go.

The bantering continued through the shift. Later that evening, I heard Adam clear a hospital on the way to the funeral home I worked at.

Me: "Say hi to the staff for me."

Adam: "It's so nice to hear a sane voice."

Me: "Thank you Adam. So kind of you to call me sane since you are so paranoid."

The job at the transfer service presented all kinds of challenges, things can go wrong and one has to maintain a positive attitude.

Perry and Adam, while on a house call, had closed the bedroom door for privacy while they transferred the deceased to the stretcher. As they prepared to leave the door knob came off. Their attempts to get it back on were futile. By now they were trying not to laugh.

The family were in the next room and the guys were conscious of the difficulty they were facing in their grief. They did their best to attract the attention of the police officer (police are called to sudden death situations) without being too obvious. After considerable delay the officer went to check on them to see what was taking so long and heard their quiet plea for help.

On another call, the same two entered the deceased's bedroom and asked the family for permission to move objects to facilitate the transfer. The family agreed and returned to the living room with the police officer. A toy train was on the bed. Perry placed it on the floor. When they were ready to leave, Adam informed the family they would be departing while Perry folded the sheets and blankets and placed them neatly at the foot of the bed. As a final gesture of respect, Perry placed the toy train back on the bed. The police officer came to the doorway of the bedroom and requested the transfer team's names for the record.

As Adam and Perry completed their chat with the officer they bent down to pick up the stretcher. The train self-activated. "Choo-choo, choo-choo, have a nice trip" is said as it chugged across the bed, smoke puffing from its stack. As suddenly as it started it stopped. A pale police officer and two spooked transfer staff made a dignified, albeit hasty retreat from the house.

Once, on my way out of base to do an out of town run, Perry asked me to help move cars so Harris could leave on a call. Harris was being quite a pest so Perry asked me to drive Harris to the Bloor viaduct and push him off. Harris commented that it was no wonder he was paranoid. I cheerfully agreed with both of them.

CHAPTER FOUR

Doughnuts and Death?

Considering the hours I was working, it was inevitable that I'd start to show the fatigue. One night I kept dozing off at the wheel on an out-of-town trip. Usually I could pull over and take a short nap, but with a body on board that wasn't possible and I had a tight schedule.

My guardian angel that night was a truck driver who followed me for quite a distance, blasting me with his air horn when my vehicle started to drift. As I got within radio range of base I called in to let them know I was about an hour out and Hummer kept me talking until I got there. He had a fresh pot of coffee on and doughnuts.

He made me rest for about fifteen minutes, then he came with me to the funeral home to deliver the deceased, only to find out we forgot the key. Back to base we went, picked up the key and delivered the body. It seemed odd wandering through a strange funeral home in the middle of the night looking for the prep room.

At 4:15 a.m. I crawled into bed, twenty hours after my day started only to begin all over again four hour later. Hummer didn't have to wait for me or get doughnuts or make coffee. He didn't have to transfer the body to the funeral home either. That level of kindness made the job so much easier.

About a month after my move to Toronto the tailor who made the funeral suits completed mine. As I put on the striped skirt, grey vest and black jacket I felt a little bit like my licenced colleagues – we all looked the same. The tailoring was impeccable, it was the first time ever I had a tailored set of clothing. It helped me feel a bit more competent. Even in the middle of the night we put our stripes on. Families don't care what time it is, they look to the funeral director for assistance and it was important to look professional.

One night at the transfer service I was placed on second call. This meant that after completing my shift I would be paged if a call requiring the assistance of a second person came in. If the person on first call was out and another call came in, it would come to me. For that reason, I elected to sleep on the couch at base. I left my suit on and tried to rest.

Before I could drift off, a coroner's call came in and Marshall and I were dispatched to the scene of a car accident. We waited quite a while for the firemen to extract the deceased from the wreckage. As we waited, Marshall noticed a crowd of spectators gathered. He got out of the vehicle and asked one of the police officers to move the crowd farther back. Climbing back into our vehicle has expressed his annoyance at the situation.

"That is someone's husband or father or son. I hate it when people stand and stare." When we transferred the body out of the vehicle he made a point of having officers stand around us to shield the deceased from onlookers.

Back at base I tried once again to go to sleep. No such luck, it was just too central. I startled one of the directors who came wandering through in his bathrobe – he didn't know I was there. The shower was just off the kitchen and it meant having to check before I went in for coffee. Just before eight a.m. I had to get up, the room became the office for the day shift.

My second time on call I tried sleeping at base again. I managed to lie down for half an hour before the first call came in. The person on first call was on a run so Debbie, who was on third call, and I set out. House calls are priority, it's important to respond within the hour. It is a very difficult time for the family and to send two women out together at night on a house call was not the best idea. There was no other staff available so we had no choice.

Driving across the city with Debbie I ignored the speed limit and drove a little faster than the law allowed, not too concerned that we'd be pulled over. Chances were we would not be ticketed if stopped, under the circumstances we'd probably just be cautioned.

We found the street after a few false turns. The building was set back quite a way from the road and there was no elevator. This meant using the two-man stretcher which was carried up and down the stairs, no wheels. The call was on the top floor. A policeman met us outside the apartment.

"Is there just the two of you?"

For a brief moment I felt guilty. We were both short and we knew that carrying a body down stairs required strength. The officer was clearly expecting two men.

"Yes, that's all. Just us," Debbie said. "Is the deceased large?"

"Well, yes," he replied. He shook his head in bewilderment. "I don't know why they would send two women. However, I can give you a hand."

"Thank you very much," Debbie said as we entered the apartment. The family were seated in the living room. I turned to greet them.

"We won't be too long. I will be back to chat with you in a few minutes." Usually upon clearing a house call we let the family know the funeral home they had chosen would be in touch the next day, we ensured they had their immediate concerns addressed.

Ideally one should be able to lift half their body weight. The variables such as stairs, height of carry, length of carrying the weight, terrain and weather all factor into it though. My partner and I could comfortably manage about 54 kg (120 lbs). Most bodies weigh more, so the officer wasn't out of line asking his question. Neither of us were particularly athletic and it was safe to say we had poor upper body strength. Both of us were students, she was applying to Humber for the following year and had moved to Toronto to work.

The deceased was on the floor, hence the police presence because of the sudden death. In low voices Debbie and I discussed the best way to expedite the removal of the body, which wasn't as large as we thought it would be. I suggested we remove our jackets.

"I can't," she whispered. "I don't have a bra on." I suppressed a snort of laughter. Rummaging for clothes in the middle of the night and getting dressed in three minutes after startling awake could lead to the occasional omission.

We hiked up our skirts to straddle the body. The seam on the bottom hem was prone to tearing, the uniform was not meant for physical work. It would have made sense if we were able to wear dress pants for transfers but that was not acceptable attire since we were representing the funeral home chosen by the family. Families didn't know we worked as agents for all the funeral homes using the service, so appearance, demeanor and protocol mattered.

"On three," I said. It couldn't have been smoother. The officer expressed his surprise. He and Debbie picked up the stretcher and headed to the door, I returned to the family to pick up the paperwork left by the coroner and answer any questions.

Debbie and the officer had just finished putting the body in the vehicle when I got downstairs. She'd given the officer our names for the record and we were free to clear the scene.

"I must admit, I'm shocked," the officer said. "I really can't believe they sent two women. Why would you want to do this?"

We explained that we were student funeral directors and agreed it was hard at times. We also told him if necessary we could radio for assistance, but usually the police officers at the scene were very helpful, and thanked him for his help.

"Well, this certainly is a first for me," he said, shaking his head. "Now I've seen everything." As we pulled away Debbie and I congratulated each other. It was the first time both of had worked with a female partner.

Women have been working in funeral service in Canada since 1919 when Violet Guymer of Manitoba became the first licenced female funeral director. She had taken over the business when her husband died.

Even though it was seventy years later it was still a challenge at times to be accepted. Personally, I don't think it matters whether you are male or female, what is important is whether or not one can do all parts of the job. Lifting was by far the hardest, there were many times I could not do it. Over and over I encountered men who used that as an excuse for women not to be in funeral service. Since ninety percent of our time was spent with the living I concentrated on being good at that part of my career, using my brain, and did my best to ignore the often ignorant remarks from my male colleagues.

In Toronto that wasn't as much of a problem as it was in the smaller towns and rural area, it was usually men my age or older who questioned our ability. A coroner's call or house call did require brute strength, something a team of women could fall short on. The police officers were often quick to offer assistance and it was, on my part, very much appreciated.

Admittedly not all transfers go smoothly. On an AIDS call one night I put on gloves to do the transfer. A nurse told my partner that she felt gloves were an extreme measure. BSP (body substance precautions) meant we wore gloves on all transfers unless the body was pouched, and in time even that didn't matter, gloves were standard. Hepatitis, meningitis, and other infectious diseases required precautions.

Another interesting job at the funeral service was airport runs – dropping off or picking up human remains. Each airline had strict protocols for the handling of human remains and the care and respect shown by air cargo staff was exemplary.

We also were required to inspect human remains for university anatomy departments. When a person donates their body to science the university may not be able to accept them. The cause of death, size of the deceased and time of death all come into play. We would inspect the body, clear it with the director on duty, and take the body to the university morgue. All identification was removed and the body was given a number. Many of our deliveries to the morgue at the university would take place in the middle of the night. It was a little eerie walking into a freezer containing enlarged body parts.

Meanwhile, back at the funeral home I was experiencing new situations. In a three week-period we did five baby funerals. For the first I picked up the tiny wrapped bundle at the hospital morgue, placed it in a leather bag and covered the little baby with a receiving blanket.

At the funeral home my boss stayed with me while I unwrapped it. Tears sprang to my ears and I tried to choke back sobs. My boss offered to take over. He did not diminish me for having feelings, he was compassionate and kind. I kept working, knowing that I would be required to work with children many times over the course of my career.

I dressed and casketed the tiny body. Usually we ask the parents if they would like to do that task. We have a change table and blankets for that purpose. If the mother is to be in hospital for a few days we wait until she is well enough to come to the funeral home. Sometimes we are able to go to her where we gather in the hospital chapel for the service.

The casket spray for this baby was made of pink and white rosebuds with baby's breath. A matching bouquet of pink and white sat beside the little casket in the chapel with a white velvet draping.

The director asked me to assist by closing the casket and carrying it to the parents in the car. A coach is not used for baby funerals. As we waited for the minister to finish, he had an idea. “Why don’t you slip up to the organ and play a lullaby or something?” he asked. As the service ended I went up the side aisle, looked up “Jesus Loves Me” in a hymn book and provided some quiet background music while the parents said their goodbyes.

I kept my head down because I was teary. It was a gentle and considerate gesture on the part of my boss. I wouldn’t have thought of it. We didn’t charge for baby funerals and for that reason we didn’t hire an organist. For a young, single man my boss showed remarkable sensitivity.

To carry a baby all those months only to have it die and have others act as functionaries seems unreasonable and cruel. Well-meaning family members think that by shielding the mom from the funeral process they are protecting her, but allowing the mom and dad to assist in preparing the child for the service and burial is an act of kindness. It allows them to work through their grief in a tangible way.

Only once did I have a couple ask me to take the baby, cremate it and dispose of it. They wanted no involvement whatsoever, they signed the forms and dismissed me. I explained that we would hold the cremated remains at the funeral home until they were ready. In their grief they brushed me off and said they wouldn't be back. Six months later they did return to pick up the cremated remains. They had worked through the shock and grief and were ready for closure.

Public trustee funerals were also a new experience. In that situation the deceased does not have family to take care of the arrangements, so the government provides the service.

One of the other students or myself took care of the details, transferring, assisting with embalming, dressing and casketing and chapel set up. We would put out the register book and place the name on the directory at the front door of the funeral home. A minister would read the service and staff would sit in the pews as mourners. We all acted as pallbearers. The coach would proceed to the cemetery, the committal read, and one of us would do the committal sand, making an X or a sign of the cross, whatever was appropriate.

Not all funeral homes put that much effort into public trustee funerals. I was grateful to be working in a funeral home where the attitude was that everyone deserved the dignity in death that those with money or family were able to provide for themselves.

Back at the transfer service I took my third night on call, this time I changed tack, going home to sleep. I had worked at the funeral home all day and spent the evening at the transfer service.

Just before midnight I took a vehicle and pager home and crawled into bed. Shortly after midnight I was jarred awake by the pager. In my stupor I couldn't immediately find it and it woke up the rest of the house. I called into base, was told it would be a coroner's call and was given the address. Four and a half minutes later I pulled out of the driveway.

The call was in an apartment building. Hummer was on first call and was waiting. We were informed by the officers on the scene that the family had been located and would be coming to identify the deceased. Sitting down to wait, the four of us chatted comfortably. The two officers were quite entertaining.

When the family arrived, my partner and I moved discretely into the hall. As Hummer put it, we didn't want to look like vultures.

At the Coroner's Office the clerk informed us we had another call pending the arrival of the coroner at the scene. We opted to go for coffee and doughnuts while we waited.

Finding a doughnut shop, we pulled into the lot. As we exited our vehicles we were startled by a gruff, "What are you doing here?" and turned to see the two officers from the call we had just completed. They joined us and over coffee we picked up the conversation we'd started earlier. Their radio went off and they headed out to their next call. We mentioned that we might see them again. How I wished that hadn't been the case.

Hummer and I were paged a short while later where we completed a house call. As we finished that one, we received another coroner's call. It was now the middle of the night and I just wanted to get some sleep.

We were dispatched to a residential area. Several blocks from the scene we were stopped by an officer, one of the two we'd worked with earlier. She had a distressed look on her face as she explained the situation. A fire had claimed a number of victims, including a baby.

We cleared the second level of security a block later and drove into the scene. A police officer approached us to tell us we would be removing the baby. The fire chief and coroner accompanied us into the house. Usually the coroner has cleared the scene by the time we arrive, for some reason he chose to stay.

I walked soberly beside Hummer who was carrying the baby case. The fire chief ensured we walked carefully once we entered the home – there wasn't much left and the building was compromised. He and the coroner led us to the baby who was charred and black. I bent down and gently started to pry it loose from the floor. One of the firemen offered to assist but I declined. He stepped back, his job completed, I had to do mine.

It was a quiet group of individuals who watched as Hummer and I wrapped the baby and closed the case. My instincts were to cradle it close, but of course I couldn't. As we left the house we were hit by a wall of lights, cameras and flashbulbs. Media personnel followed us to the car. I could feel my anger rise. One persistent reporter jostled me as I was putting the baby case in the vehicle asking questions.

Turning to the police officer who walked out with us I said in a very low voice through gritted teeth, "Would you please get rid of that jerk." He quickly directed the reporter to the spokesperson for the fire department.

We were not allowed to speak with reporters while on duty at the transfer service, ever. At the funeral home that could be a remote possibility but not on a coroner's call. The reporter could not have known that. My reaction was about the baby, not the reporter, although he could have been more respectful.

My sister was a reporter in another part of the country and I understood her point of view and how her job worked. I recognized that I'd have to learn not to let the media affect me.

The summer was drawing to a close. By now I was getting comfortable driving coach and flower cars. Observing other directors at work helped me develop a consistent style. Even stance made a difference, standing up straight with your hands behind your back forces you into alertness. A sloppy, slouching person looks and acts as if they're not interested. Maybe the family doesn't notice but if a director takes pride in his or her work by paying attention to details, the staff will follow suit.

I made the decision to work only at the transfer service once school started. My boss, the training director at the funeral home, was moving on in his career and had accepted a position at one of the larger funeral homes in the city. I was very happy for him and we agreed to stay in touch.

He not only taught me how to do things, he showed me the joy of doing them, such as setting up for a Buddhist funeral. The beauty of the alter with a fresh flower, incense, fruit and candle embodied the simplicity of the Buddhist faith. The cultural mosaic of Toronto meant learning about faith, death and life and he was well versed in all of it.

Work at the transfer service meant long hard hours but the experience was invaluable. I had opportunities that many directors might not see in their careers.

One call came from out of town. The service was asked to repatriate a prominent person who had come to Canada on vacation. His sudden death was a tremendous shock to his wife. She did not speak English and was understandably confused and frightened. The ambassador from her country had called her from Ottawa to offer assistance.

When my partner and I arrived at the hotel we were not too sure what we'd encounter. As we entered the hotel, our pagers went off. However, we had to assess this call before moving on to the next one.

We were met at the door of the hotel room by a charming lady who served as a translator. She informed us that their culture dictated that the family stay with the body for several hours after death. My partner and I exchanged glances.

Since both our pages beeped simultaneously we knew we had a house call or a coroner's call to respond to and we had to be there within the hour. While my partner talked with the translator I excused myself to find a telephone.

The pending call was a homicide. We were given explicit instructions to proceed to the scene as quickly as possible. When I re-entered the hotel room I took my partner aside and we discussed the best way to expedite the two calls. It seemd logical to allow the wife more time with her husband and proceed to the homicide. We could then return to the hotel.

The translator had other ideas however. She wanted to go home as she had been with the family all day. Another few hours was too much for her. It was approaching midnight.

The widow was wandering aimlessly back and forth, confused and frightened. As she passed me I caught her eye and held her gaze. I touched her arm gently. Like a drowning person she clutched my arm and held on. The non-verbal communication let me 'tell' her that I did care about her husband even though I couldn't speak her language and I was a stranger.

She held on to me while she and the translator exchanged information. Occasionally she would glance at me for reassurance. I could only nod and give her arm a reassuring squeeze.

Ten minutes later we left the room with the deceased. A memento from the wife had been placed in his hands and she seemed relieved to let him go.

It would take a few days to ship the body to her country where they would be reunited. The director at the transfer service would ensure that the memento would be in his hands after the embalming and before placing him in the shipping container. It seems the custom of staying with the body was not as important as she had first emphasized. I think she needed to know that we'd take good care of her beloved partner, and until she had that reassurance she was reluctant to let him go. It took a team, the ambassador, translator and us to let her know he would be safe.

With about four minutes to spare we arrived at the homicide – an entirely different scenario. There was no gentleness or softness there. Two scruffy-looking, large, burly men met us. The guns on their belts identified them as officers. The deceased was young, the same age as my daughter. He'd been shot in a drug-related execution.

The undercover officers were used to dealing with such homicides and they were all business. We worked at that scene quickly, no family to talk to or reassure.

We put the body in a pouch and one of the officers placed a seal on it. My partner took his vehicle to the coroner's office, one of the officers rode with him. There was only room for two, so his partner rode with me.

If a death is a suspected homicide, an officer has to ride in the vehicle with the deceased to ensure that no one tampers with the evidence on the body.

The officer who rode with me was pleasant and suggested we stop and pick up coffee and doughnuts for everyone, they'd been on the scene for hours. He laid his revolver on the seat between us. We sped up, pulled over the transfer vehicle and asked what they wanted in their coffee. The officer stayed in my car while I fetched the food. Once the other two were done, we sat down over coffee and chatted.

A short while later we were dispatched on a house call. The address was on the other side of the city. It took a bit of time to get there, over the required hour because the funeral home had given the dispatcher at the answering service the wrong address.

We had to drive to the funeral home, wake up the director again, and get the right address. When we finally arrived at the home, the family doctor met us at the door.

"Did you bring the medical certificate?" he asked

The word no was barely out of my mouth before he exploded in anger.

“I told you people to bring the medical certificate. What’s the matter with you?” The family was standing behind him.

“If you will excuse me sir, I will be right back,” and I turned back to my vehicle. We had not been notified that a medical certificate was required, usually the doctors or coroners carry them. I could hear the doctor continuing to express his outrage to the family. Paul was waiting at the van.

“That’s another mix-up we didn’t need tonight,” he said. “Bad enough that the funeral home didn’t get the address right, they could have at least told us the doctor needed a medical certificate. I would have put in my pocket.”

I located a blank medical form in the glove box and took it to the physician. By this time, he’d run out of steam. He asked us to wait, and filled it out at the door. Handing me the completed form he picked up one end of the stretcher, told me to stand back and took over.

Paul and the doctor proceeded to put the deceased on the stretcher backwards. Paul could see the problem but he wisely chose not to say anything in front of the family. The doctor watched Paul push the stretcher into the back of the van. Pushing it backwards made the task difficult because one end of the stretcher has wheels, the other metal legs so one can be anchored. The legs screeched across the metal floor of the van as Paul pushed the stretcher in. We pretended we didn't hear it and acted like nothing had happened. We drove away very slowly because the stretcher wasn't anchored and it takes very little to bang and bump around. At least the doctor had tried to help.

Meanwhile, I had a bone to pick with the funeral director who'd given us the wrong address and not passed along instructions about the blank certificate. A lot of time had been wasted because he didn't give the correct information.

Arriving at the funeral home we were surprised to find the back entrance unlocked. We didn't have to use our key and the alarm was off. After we placed the body in the prep room and got it ready for the directors for the next day, we left the building. Only this time we did trigger the alarm. That didn't make sense. Paul looked at me.

"Should we stay and face the music or should we leave?" he asked. I hesitated. I'd had enough for one night but something didn't add up. The funeral home should not have been open at two in the morning. Why would the alarm go off when we left? Looking around the parking lot we saw a parked car with a scruffy looking character slouched down in the driver's seat.

"Paul, look at that. What is he doing there?" Funeral homes are vulnerable for theft, the deceased being a target in the suites, their jewelry easy to remove and pocket. We knew the police would be arriving shortly to check out the alarm. We threw caution to the wind. In retrospect, we should have had more sense but one gets caught up in the drama of the moment and we were tired, and making stupid mistakes. Paul and I hopped into the station wagon and drove up to the car. Rolling down my window I confronted the man.

"Are you waiting to see a funeral director?" I asked. Stupid question actually. In Toronto most funeral homes make appointments with families for the next day, since the transfer service takes care of the immediate details if there is a night call.

This guy was not dressed for a visit to the funeral home. He looked at us and reached into his jacket. For a brief second my heart stopped. I was just two feet away. I found myself staring at a police badge.

"Oh," I said exhaling. Are you here in response to the alarm?

"No. I'm on robbery detail. There have been a number of break-ins in this area." Paul and I looked at each other.

"You may have another one," Paul said. "The funeral home was open and there was no one around."

"Let's check it out," he replied. He radioed for backup which arrived quickly and we headed into the funeral home. The four of us wandered through the basement and the selection room looking for intruders. We went up to the main floor and started checking the suites when we her footsteps coming down the hall. A sleepy person in boxer shorts jumped when the officer confronted him. I recognized him as one of the directors from previous calls to that funeral home.

"Can I help you?" he said crossly. The policeman was all business. He pulled out his badge and asked for identification. The funeral director stood there and stared dumbly at the officer through his sleepy haze.

Since the director was dressed only in boxer shorts it did seem like a foolish question. I could feel a chuckle bubble inside. The funeral director looked past him and recognized me.

"These people know who I am," he said. My chuckle escaped and I laughed. I wanted to say the classic "Officer, I've never seen this man before in my life" but instead I reassured the policeman that it was OK.

We explained to the funeral director why we'd come back in. The funeral director explained he'd unlocked the door as we pulled up and accidently reset the alarm thinking we had departed. The director was as short of sleep as we were and had not wakened with a full deck.

I chided him gently for sending us to the wrong address, but told him I understood. We had a good laugh over the mix-up, said goodnight, and headed for the parking lot. There were four more policemen in the parking lot outside, more back up.

On the way back to base our pagers went off again. We were dispatched to the forensic centre at the coroner's office to remove two bodies from a burned vehicle. It was my first experience in the forensic centre and I braced myself for what I knew could be a traumatic experience.

Clearing the double security doors, we pulled into the underground garage where vehicles that have been involved in fatalities and were under investigation were stored. A flatbed truck was parked outside the first set of doors. We were met by an Ontario Provincial Police officer from across the province. The car he had escorted to Toronto was charred and black. The victims were not yet identified. They were burned beyond recognition, it was impossible to determine their age or sex.

Our job was to remove the remains from the vehicle and transport them upstairs to the coroner's office. It was a grim and difficult removal. There was only room for one of us to work at a time. Paul and I didn't speak except to discuss the best way to remove the victims. It was very dirty work, our funeral suits were covered with soot.

We used crowbars to pry away the twisted metal. It affected both of us deeply and our voices were low and subdued. Finally, Paul voiced our sentiment.

"I hope they didn't suffer," he said. The OPP officer overhead us.

"We don't think they did. The explosion engulfed the car in seconds. They were too far from town for the fire department to get there in time."

Apparently, there was a defect in the gas tank, resulting in a rare situation – a sudden explosion. That model of car had been recalled years before, there were very few left on the road.

Once we started talking about how horrified we were by this accident the task seemed more humane, more personal. I had a bad moment when I found what we thought was a small child in the back seat but experienced a huge sense of relief when we realized it was a large turkey, the two individuals had been bringing groceries home.

It took us two and a half hours to free the first body. I transported it in the service car out of the garage and around the building to the coroner's office upstairs. The OPP officer rode with me and stayed until I placed the body in storage. We went back down to help Paul finish. The sun was shining brightly when we took the second body up. We were saddened and retrospective.

"Kind of makes you think about your own death, doesn't it," Paul said.

I concurred.

CHAPTER FIVE

No Time to Party

The last week in August, Humber College held an Orientation Day for the Health Sciences Programs. It was our first look at our fellow funeral directors-to-be, about one hundred and thirty-five in all – a rather conservative looking group.

The day was well-organized. Our class was divided into four groups of thirty-three. We met the faculty, picked up our timetables and had our ID picture taken. The pictures were taken in the lab, we sat on the preparation table. For those students who had never seen a preparation room that must have been a bit disconcerting.

It was a quiet group that assembled for instructions after lunch. The class I was in wasn't exactly lively, and most of the instructor's attempts at levity fell flat. We were all so intense, and concerned that we wouldn't make the grade or that we'd get off on the wrong foot and have to leave, that we were unresponsive to humour.

Waiting in the line for our timetables was a tall pretty girl. We said hello and asked each other where we were from. It turned out that we were living a few blocks away from one another in the east end, about an hour's drive from Humber. We agreed to ride together. It was the beginning of a strange and strong friendship.

Over the school year we were inseparable. She was smart but had received little exposure to the practical aspects of funeral service. I had to work hard for every mark but had the practical experience. We agreed to disagree on everything relating to news, politics and taste in music as we could not have been more opposite. She loved to party, I hated it. She was athletic, I didn't do sports. Together we balanced out one another – the weaknesses in our studies and perspectives on life.

The first day of school I picked her up two hours before our first class. The traffic warranted such an early departure and parking at the college was limited. Although we thought two hours would be more than enough time to get to a 9 a.m. class, we were wrong. It took two hours just to get to the college and another hour to park.

There was a shuttle bus service from the overflow parking but it couldn't keep up with the demand. The thought of leaving every morning at 6 a.m. wasn't very appealing. Fortunately, over time parking eased up and we settled into a reasonable routine.

During orientation class our first week, our instructor told us to look at the person on our right and left. He said that one out of every three of us would be a 'Christmas graduate', they would flunk out. We looked around. I knew I would have to find or form a study group to be successful.

The first week was intimidating. In each new class the instructor cautioned us about study habits and the failure rate. The question "what is embalming?" was asked of us over and over. The answer: embalming is the disinfection, preservation and restoration of a dead human body with disinfection being the primary reason for embalming.

We were instructed on what to wear to school. The dress code was to reflect the image we portrayed as funeral directors, no track pants or sketchy clothing. On field trips we were to act with dignity and maturity and most importantly, we were not to discuss anything related to our lab or embalming in the hallways of the college. The result of such an infraction was immediate dismissal.

The mature students over twenty-five years of age were asked to stay behind. About one-third of the class fit that category. The faculty gave us a pep talk, encouraging us to get help early if we were struggling and letting us know that our chances of success in the program were high because of our maturity. We were not as likely to goof off and party. As it turned out my social life was non-existent. If I wasn't working I was studying, if I wasn't studying I was sleeping. That became my routine and I loved it.

A notice was posted on the board about a mature student get together. The instructors approached us individually as well and asked us to attend. The Associate Dean was present as well as the head of the counselling department. Coffee and muffins were served. We were welcomed to Humber and told what services were available to us.

We introduced ourselves and talked about our previous careers, jobs and families. Several of the students were laughing about their timetable mix-ups. They thought LANG 101 was the name of the instructor and the room number and could not find the class. LANG 101 was the communications course.

Another person introduced himself as a recent high school graduate, thirty-seven years ago. It was an encouraging afternoon and I left feeling a little less overwhelmed. I wasn't the only parent who'd left home, there were three of us.

Three days into the course a notice on the board informed us that all classes were cancelled for a general lab. This meant that we were to watch an embalming. Some of us had seen one before and we chose to sit in classrooms adjacent to the lab and watch it on the TV monitors. The majority of students crowded into the gallery above the preparation room. The advantage to being in the classroom meant we could slip out for coffee and we could sit down. The lab lasted about four and a half hours.

My friend and I were asked to guard the locked classroom door. Students in other programs were known to try to sneak in to see the dead body and embalming. We'd been drilled over and over about dignity and respect and she and I were to be the guardians of the deceased that day.

The lab was intense and we were bombarded with information such as the types of coagulation after death, what guidelines to use in fluid preparation, maximum index, etc. It was a very clinical presentation with an overload of information.

We were told that if the family wanted a closed casket we were to prepare the body as if it were to be open. The instructor shared a story about a funeral director who did not put the viscera (organs) back into the autopsied body he'd prepared, he placed them in a bag in the foot of the casket. In one case, he forgot so he put the bag into the casket of the next deceased person. For medical/legal reasons that was serious enough, let alone the moral implications.

The main purpose of embalming, disinfection, was also a focal point of the lab presentation. A dead body is full of bacteria. So is a live one but our body has checks and balances to control it. If the family and mourners are demonstrative in kissing the deceased they can be exposed to a variety of pathogens. Preservation and restoration follow. The whole point of embalming is not to make the deceased look like they are sleeping. They are not sleeping, they are dead.

The second general lab took place the following day, this time with an autopsied body. Again, my friend and I sat in the classroom and watched the door.

Our first semester courses consisted of Anatomy and Physiology, Microbiology (with an emphasis on post mortem effects of bacteria and concurrent and terminal disinfection), Moral and Ethical Issues in Health, Humanities, Orientation (the practical part of funeral service), Communications, Embalming Lab and Embalming Theory.

I had received exemptions from Anatomy and Physiology, Microbiology, Com-munications and Humanities. I chose to audit Anatomy and Physiology and Microbiology because I felt the refresher wouldn't hurt when it came time to take Pathology in second semester.

We were asked to form groups of four. It was a careful selection process, people were looking for fellow students who seemed reliable and smart. Lab was a tough course.

In addition to class time we were pulled out of classes for a day to embalm. This took place twice a semester and we had to change groups each time.

With thirty people in our section that meant we would work closely with seven other people. If someone in the lab group wasn't doing their share we could fire them. They then had to do their own lab and would receive the minimum grade of sixty percent.

Our group submitted our names to the program office the first week of school. Our strategy was to get one lab over with before midterms. My friend and I picked two guys to work with us on our first lab. We solicited help from another classmate to get notes from the classes we would miss that day so we could catch up and reciprocated with them.

In our first lab we were allowed to take in a pen and paper to record the information but for the remaining three labs over the year that was not allowed, it had to be committed to memory.

The bodies were donated from Social Services, indigents who were unclaimed by family or from a participating funeral home in Toronto.

The third week of school our lab dates were posted. Our team was scheduled for the following week. We would enter the lab at 9 a.m. The door was always locked. Funeral services students were free to come and observe, visitors to the lab such as Health Science instructors or a visiting funeral director were limited when preparation was taking place.

Lab day we had a hearty breakfast, we did not have breaks or lunch unless it was for health reasons such as diabetes. We donned plastic aprons, shoes covers, head covers and gloves. Every procedure was closely supervised as we followed instructions.

After placing the body on the preparation table we removed the shroud, rolling it away from us carefully and disposing of it in the biohazardous waste box. The privacy of the deceased was respected by covering the genital area. The body was washed with a disinfectant. Even that became clinical. On a test we had to explain that the disinfectant soap was used to remove as many surface pathogens as possible by chemically destroying them and physically washing them away.

The cause of death was discussed. Depending on the cause and length of time from death to embalming and embalming to final disposition, different fluid strengths and types are used. In our first lab we were told what fluid solution to use. In most cases a pre-injection can be used to expand

and clear the vascular system. Our case warranted a pre-injection. We were shown how to disinfect and set the facial features and what form of mouth closure to use. The instructor raised the carotid artery (injection) and jugular vein (drainage).

We watched for signs of fluid distribution, massaging the extremities to assist with distribution. Very seldom did one stay with a one-point injection in lab, we usually had to raise other vessels as well.

We would also use various drainage techniques. Aspiration of the abdominal cavity was performed by each team member under close scrutiny of the instructor. The incisions were sutured and the body washed and dried. This process averaged five hours.

Once the body was transferred to the stretcher terminal disinfection of the lab started, another two hour process. Even the army wasn't that fussy. Bacteria didn't have a chance.

We were marked on attitude, for example, how we responded when asked to rewash the cupboard doors for the third time. The instruments were washed and sterilized twice. Our attitude towards our team mates was noted. By four-thirty we passed final inspection and left the lab, tired and hungry.

The lab report had to be submitted within ten school days of the embalming. That meant we worked after school as a group to compile, analyze and research the information needed to put together the sixty-five-page report. Every spare minute was spent on that report and spare minutes were hard to come by.

The case analysis made up the bulk of the report which covered the intrinsic and extrinsic variables of our case. Our first report did not go into the details of the chemicals in the fluids we used, that knowledge would come in time so we were exempt from that part, but it did outline the reasons and effects of the fluid selection.

Each lab group had to present their lab report during the two-hour class allotted for that purpose. Our group was to present after midterms. Once the lab report was handed in, I put it out of my mind and concentrated on essays and papers. Classes were usually lectures. Some classes such as Orientation meant three hours of lectures and notes had to be tidied up for studying.

Since some of the evenings and all my weekends were spent working, there wasn't a lot of free time. I learned to compile and sort information quickly.

My husband and children came for a weekend visit in the early fall. I was on shift and call that weekend and had worked from early morning to nearly eleven p.m. I arrived home, chatted for about ten minutes and fell into bed, exhausted. Ten minutes later my pager went off and I wasn't to see them again before they went home. We decided that regular trips to Toronto were futile, it would be several months before I would see them again.

Shortly before midterms the anatomy professor asked to see me. I had missed auditing several classes to use the time to catch on my credit courses. Auditing was an added challenge, I was exhausted and it was hard to maintain my concentration.

The anatomy professor was a very kind and compassionate man who was well-respected by the students. He told us he liked teaching the funeral service students because they worked so hard. We chatted for a few minutes before he got to the reasons he had asked me to come in.

Several of the students in funeral service were struggling and he suggested I tutor them. He was prepared to write a letter to the peer tutoring office recommending me. I groaned inwardly. He explained that peer tutors were paid. Part of being in funeral service meant helping our colleagues but I didn't feel qualified to tutor.

I recalled my response when we were told about the dropout rate and how I thought studying together would help. I was being asked to practice what I preached. He listened to my protests patiently but refused to accept them, encouraging me to give it a try.

There had yet to be a funeral service peer tutor, I was to become the first. I agreed to meet with the peer tutoring office.

After my meeting with the peer tutoring counsellor I felt a little better about helping the students who were struggling. It meant I could cut back on my week nights at the transfer service.

One more letter of recommendation was required and I approached John Finn. He suggested I wait until my mid-term marks were in. I didn't quite know how to read that. John then asked me to come into his office and sit down. In class he was all business but outside the classroom he showed a gentler, less intimidating side.

"How are things?" he asked. He mentioned he'd observed me leaving the college in the removal vehicle when the transfer service would pick up the embalmed bodies after lab and transport them to their respective funeral homes.

I used that system to get to work, my friend took the car home and picked me up for school the next day. He showed genuine interest and I dropped my guard, opening up about my family, how hard it was working evenings and weekends and how I missed them.

I left his office about half an hour later feeling much differently than I did going in. I realized I'd been trying too hard to make the right impression. It really didn't matter. The instructors had something I wanted – the knowledge to get my licence. I was learning something else. We were becoming a close-knit group with common interests and needs. My classmates were like family and the professors helped foster that bond.

During midterms, the air was palpable with tension. Essentially the first semester tests were regurgitation of information. The second semester would require more application on what we'd learned. Several students left before the week was over, the information overload too much for them. John gave me the letter for the peer tutoring office as soon as my midterms were graded.

Just after midterms a list of awards was posted which encompassed the first and second year students. My friend and I scanned the list with interest.

There were technical awards for embalming excellence, various academic awards covering the sciences and professional subjects, and awards for students who showed potential and improvement. There was even an award for the first-year student who showed the concern and compassion by assisting fellow students in personal and academic endeavours.

Turning to my friend I remarked, “If I could pick any award, it would be that one.” I knew she would be receiving academic awards, she was a top student. There was an award for the student with the best sense of humour – more than one qualified for that!

Once midterms ended we concentrated on our lab group presentation. Funeral service students were required to up the dress code for field trips, speeches and presentations. Looking the part instilled some credibility into our presentation.

The class dutifully took notes while we presented. I gave the case analysis. John asked us questions after each section. Even though we were well-prepared, if we correctly answered a question John would increase the level of difficulty.

"What is putrefaction?" John asked me after I had answered my first question correctly.

"Uh, the chemical process and decay that appears first in the abdomen," I replied.

"That's not what I asked," said John. "What is putrefaction?"

"I don't know," I wisely responded. I knew I couldn't answer. He asked each of my lab partners. They fumbled too.

"Putrefaction and decay are two entirely different things. Putrefaction is the anaerobic breakdown of complex body protein into unstable compounds accompanied by odour. Decay is aerobic," he responded.

It did not seem to matter how much preparation went into your lab. John used the opportunity to teach us that we could never know it all and instilled in us the need to keep learning after graduation.

We were relieved when the two hours ended. Our lab group went to John's office to get our mark. He explained the weakness and strength of the report and pointed out our contradictions. We were given a B. Lab was a tough course, it was almost impossible to get an A.

The purpose of the lab presentation was to produce an effective communicator. It is important to give details and pay attention to details because a funeral is a combination of little things. If one falls down it produces a domino effect.

The presentation addressed the issue of teamwork as well, and it could mean sharing marks with a lab partner who may not have pulled their full weight. A funeral service requires the combined efforts of at least three or more people. The presentation helped us as students to develop a sense of presence, important when, as I recalled, directing six pallbearers to move a casket from the funeral home to the coach to the church to the graveside smoothly and with dignity.

In our Orientation class we learned how to do removals. We were shown the correct way to lift and we talked about various techniques and how to handle difficult situations. Our professor informed us that our next class would be practical, we would use the one man and two man stretchers, strap in a classmate and practice on the stairs. We had watched the ambulance students do the same with their stretchers, and laughed as they occasionally careened down the halls with their "patients".

After class the professor asked to see me. Since I had a bit more experience than most of the students, because of my, job would I mind working with the girls to teach them a few techniques? I jumped at the chance. Working at the transfer service had been a negative experience on a few occasions and I was happy to talk to the girls in the class about how to present themselves without compromising their femininity and how to deal with challenging co-workers.

The next morning on my way back from the cafeteria with a coffee I saw a group of funeral service students barrelling merrily down the hall racing one man stretchers with classmates on them. People stopped and stared. At least they hadn't zipped up the body bag all the way. It was a good thing too that no one reported them.

In our next Orientation class we were shown how to strap our classmate into a stretcher. We were asked to leave the classmates hands free in case we dropped them. He asked two of the guys to carry a two man stretcher up the stairs. The class was quietly watching as the two fellows stooped down to pick up the stretcher. An audible tearing sound rent the air as one the fellows bent down. The class erupted with laughter as he backed up against the wall. Red-faced he joined in the laughter. "I guess I won't be going to next class," he said as he backed out the door.

I took the girls aside. Since many funeral homes required directors to wear funeral suits at all times I spoke to them about asking the tailor to put an inside pocket in their jacket, where they could discretely put the medical certificate.

Purses are a nuisance, I never took one to work, they could not be carried into the church or be brought to the graveside or into the hospital or on a house call. I suggested they wear flat shoes for transfers. Usually a high heel was worn for services and visitation.

It wasn't my place to preach, and I told them so, but I did suggest that swearing was inappropriate. Not all males liked doing transfers with females. I had experienced that first hand many times, and I warned the girls that just because their male partner or staff person was rude or ignorant or being a misogynist that reciprocating with innuendoes, coarse language or suggestive remarks was uncalled for.

I reminded them that if they had to hike up their skirts a little bit to facilitate a lift they should excuse themselves. I suggested they be pleasant and respectful to police officers at the scene. I told them about one of the girls I had worked with. When he politely asked her how long she'd been doing her job, her response had been "since you were born" – an unnecessary, rude and sarcastic remark.

"That attitude hurts all of us," I said. I explained that when attending a scene with police officers present we should greet the officers pleasantly. If caught in traffic and late, apologize. By the time the transfer service or funeral director arrives at a scene the officer has usually been there for hours. I would sometimes tell the officers we would do our best to finish up quickly so they could leave for lunch or supper. It certainly isn't pleasant sitting with a dead body for hours.

Not once at a scene did I have to ask for assistance, the officers always offered to help. I explained that in the event I ever did have to ask for help I would, an ambulance crew would do the same. The girls listened intently. I then showed them how to use a sheet to get a body out of a tight spot.

The professor had been listening off and on and asked if I would give the guys the same pep talk.

All but a couple were attentive. I reminded them to act like gentlemen. If their female partner was struggling I suggested they put the stretcher down and rest if the situation allowed it. Over and over I had heard from male staff that women can't lift and shouldn't be in the business. I told them to keep those kinds of remarks to themselves, it was counterproductive to a viable working relationship. As I excused myself and lifted my skirt to straddle the "body" one of the guys snickered, "Nice legs."

I turned around and confronted him. "That is exactly what I mean," I said to the group. He recoiled.

"Can't take a joke?" he grumbled.

"That was no joke," I said and turned back to what we'd been doing. The guys became a little quieter.

Some of the guys didn't want to move the stretcher so I picked the largest student, made him the "body" and watched them struggle. Stepping in I sweetly asked if they would like a hand. The rest of the fellows snickered and that ended the nonsense. I tried to keep it light, telling one of them to find a place to drop dead so we could use a sheet to move him.

I reinforced the importance of teamwork and reminded them to never criticize their partner in front of others. I told them that while on a removal my partner had remarked to a policeman, "She's a nice lady, but she can't lift." No matter how upset I was with my partner's mistakes or attitude I would save my concern until we were alone. Most of the time I let it go. You can't repair the world.

Several of the girls and I approached one the fellows after class. His dad owned a funeral home and he was well versed in procedures. "You are a gentleman," we said. "And it would be a pleasure to work with you anytime." I overheard the guy I had corrected after class say "Who does she think she is – what a bitch." He was one of the 'Christmas graduates'.

A few weeks after midterms I contracted bronchitis. Funds were tight and I didn't fill my antibiotic prescription. The coughing and general malaise wore me down. Finally I swallowed my pride and went to the program office. There was money available to students for such emergencies and I applied. Paul listened sympathetically and handed fifty dollars out of his own pocket. I assured I would repay the money as expeditiously as possible and filled the prescription.

Several days later Paul called me into his office. He asked me to sign a form, which I did without reading it.

"Don't you want to know what you signed?" he asked cheerfully. I looked at him with a rather dull expression. He handed me a cheque with my name on it. It took a few seconds to register. I don't know when I will be able to pay this back," I said.

"You don't have to, it's bursary money," he replied. My eyes were stinging and after a heartfelt thank you I beat a hasty retreat. His insight and thoughtfulness by providing the bursary made it possible for me to complete my first year.

The bursary fund was provided by anonymous funeral homes to assist students experiencing financial difficulty. I wrote a thank you not that night expressing my gratitude. It was tough at times and I appreciated not just the financial support but the emotional support of the faculty and my classmates.

The rest of the semester flew by. I had started peer tutoring immediately after midterms, a symbiotic relationship that benefitted both of us. For the most part, rounding up my charges to sit down over anatomy or microbiology could be challenging. I remember two of them on roller blades gleefully skating around me in circles refusing to work on studies that day, preferring to be outside enjoying the weather. Like little kids they told me if I could catch them they would come in.

As finals drew near I once again eased up on my work at the transfer service, using the time to study. I was booked to work over Christmas and New Year's and I would more than make up the hours.

Our second lab was uneventful and while it entailed a lot of commitment, our team worked smoothly together. We presented quietly to John instead of our class and received the same mark as the first, a B.

Finals were even more tense than midterms. Some students left the exams in tears. We were aware that many would not be back in January. Some decided funeral service was just not for them and changed programs.

One of the young women I was tutoring told me she would not be returning after Christmas. Funeral service was not her choice of career. she had tried it thinking it might be something she wanted to do and recognized she would not be happy. I gave her a hug as I wished her all the very best.

Several days after exams I called in for my marks. They weren't too bad, even Theory. The professor talked to me about next semester, advising me to cut my work hours. Lab groups in second semester required a greater effort and the team members would not tolerate less than complete dedication.

The workload was greater, I was not exempt for any subjects. He was the voice of reason and he didn't pussyfoot. I appreciated his honesty and agreed that compliance would be wise. I knew deep down that the next four months would make or break me.

They almost broke me.

CHAPTER SIX

Never Enough Sleep

Working at the funeral directors service over Christmas and New Years meant long hours. When I chose to take the position upon my move to Toronto it was for the experience. Once I graduated it was my plan to look for a quieter environment.

While employed there, I wanted to experience all I could. I kept a diary of the situations, writing down information after a call or on a break, looking up information about a disease or using it to reflect. Many nights I slept for too few hours and some nights not at all.

I had learned first term not to take call on Sunday evenings because calls could hold me up and make me late for class on Monday morning. I took advantage of the services' runs to and from the College and rode in or out with the bodies to get to class or work.

One afternoon I delivered two bodies to Humber as part of my shift. Paul offered to help. I politely declined and efficiently and smoothly removed each stretcher.

"Gee, you do that like a pro," Paul said to me and I grinned. I had come a long way from that first trip to Humber. I had lost twenty pounds and was stronger.

I really enjoyed the out of town runs. Working alone, driving around the province gave me time to think. I could log up to a thousand kilometers (approximately 620 miles) per weekend or three kilometers on a school night. I also enjoyed parking lot duty at funeral homes, another job where I was alone.

It was winter and I put a track suit on under my funeral suit to stay warm. My long black coat and boots hide the fleecy warm clothing. Parking lot duty was usually pretty uneventful.

Death during the holiday season is hard on families and it reflected back on us. Harry and I were dispatched on a house call where a body had been in a bathtub for five days. Bodies in warm water or room temperature water bloat and decompose quickly and are referred to as "floaters". It is the gas that makes bodies in lakes and rivers rise to the surface. Often the bathroom would be too small for two of us to work together. Because of the decomposition the remains had to be handled gently.

As we exited the apartment elevator a familiar stench assaulted our nostrils. A police officer let us in. Coffee was burning on the stove, a technique used to cover the odor of decomposition. Harry did most of the work since there was not enough room for the two of us. He juggled the body onto the ledge of the bathtub and dropped it onto a sheet on the floor. Together we pulled the sheet into the living room, transferred it to the pouch and took it to the Coroner's office.

A few days later one of the pathology assistants at the Coroner's office met me as I was bringing in another body. He put his arm around my shoulder.

"The next time you drop a body, let us know," he said. I looked at him in bewilderment. He went on to explain that the body we had brought in from the bathtub had fractures, all post-mortem. I was horrified. He reassured me that it was not uncommon, osteoporosis predisposes a person to pathological fractures. The drop from the edge of the tub was far enough to cause the decomposing bones to break. One does their best, had two of us been able to work side by side it might not have happened. I still felt bad about it, although the pathology clerk kept it light and teased me every time our paths crossed.

Large bodies are a problem for anyone moving them. One body of about two hundred and fifty pounds was all I could handle in one shift, and that was in optimum circumstances such as a transfer from stretcher to stretcher. Getting the stretcher into the van meant taking a bit of a run for it.

If I had two on a shift, I would be done in from wrestling with the dead weight. My worst experience involved a body somewhere in the four-hundred-pound range. I asked for assistance, no one was available. It was an out of town transfer and it meant another person couldn't be spared. I was praying there would be someone at the funeral home to assist.

No such luck. A lady let me into the funeral home. She lived above the funeral home, her job was to answer the phones and let people like me in. I asked her if there was anyone available. She explained they were either off or on a funeral. She couldn't reach anyone.

I somehow managed to get the stretcher out of the car and into the preparation room. The prep table was about six inches higher than the stretcher and it could not be lowered. There was a portable lift used to transfer bodies from the stretcher to the table. I was getting shaky. It had taken me a bit of time just to get the stretcher to the prep room since the weight of the body threw it off balance. All my movements were slow and deliberate. I studied the lift, trying to decide the best place to put the straps.

Clearly, I could not place a strap under the neck because of the risk of fracture from hyperextending the neck. Sliding it under the shoulders could cause the stretcher to tip because the body was hanging over both sides, but I had no choice.

Placing the straps took almost an hour. Had the body tipped it would have crashed to the floor, injuring me. Once the straps were placed I stood back to inspect the placement. The lift was cranked by hand.

Very slowly I started to lift the body, stopping to adjust the straps as I went. I kept the stretcher in position in case something let go. It did, the lift base itself tipped. The body landed on the stretcher which also tipped. As the lift crashed to the floor, the end of the stretcher tipped downwards. Like it was on a slide, the body slid slowly and smoothly to the floor. I lunged to try to stop it and landed on the floor partially under the body.

While it hurt, nothing of mine was broken or bleeding, I was just bruised. I was mad though, very mad. I slowly untangled myself, collapsed the stretcher to the floor and wrestled with the body, trying to get it the few inches up onto the stretcher. It was no use. My energy was spent and I stamped my foot in childish frustration, tears trickling down my cheeks.

Once I regained my composure, I tracked down the receptionist and asked her to phone someone for help. It took quite a while before she found someone, who called for more people. It took four of us to get the body onto the table. My apology was graciously accepted by the funeral director. Accidents happen. No one wants to drop a body, let alone admit it. Nor should anyone go on a transfer such as that one alone.

When I returned to base I confronted the director on duty. He'd received a call from the funeral home scolding him for not finding the staff to work with me, he in turn told them they should have been prepared at their end. Frankly, I should have refused to go by myself. I was lucky I wasn't hurt.

Once in a while I would be the senior person on call and it would be up to me to teach the new person. One day a new fellow, Ron, and I met up, left his vehicle behind and proceeded to the house call. We were met at the door by a family member. We identified ourselves and the gentleman let us in. His first words were, "I don't want embalming."

"No problem," I replied. "Do you have an appointment with a funeral home?" Under the Act written permission must be obtained from the family before a body can be embalmed so I wasn't too concerned.

"Yes," he replied. "This afternoon. But I don't want embalming." He led us to the bedroom and asked if he could help. We allowed him to find his level of involvement and he and Ron placed the body in the van.

Leaving Ron to stay with the deceased, I went back to the house to get the clothing and dentures and death certificate. The gentleman once again reiterated that he didn't want embalming. I hesitated. Obviously he felt strongly about the matter and assumed I was one of the funeral home staff.

I let him talk. He wanted to remember his wife just as she was. He expressed some misgivings about viewing the body in the funeral home.

"What do you think?" he asked. It was not my place to influence him. I chose my words carefully.

"I think it is important that your wishes are respected. Sometimes family may wish to view the body. In that case we ask they come into the funeral home before receiving friends and spend a few minutes with the casket open. When you are ready, the funeral director will close it. If you have pictures you want placed in the room, bring them with you.

He had been listening intently. "What a great idea," he said. "There are a few family members from out of town who might like that." I reassured the gentleman that the funeral home would do as he wished and said goodbye.

As I walked down the steps I glanced around. A few neighbours were standing watching. As I walked down the driveway I hit a small patch of ice. My feet shot out from under me and I landed on my back on the driveway.

Like watching a slow motion scene in a movie I watched the false teeth sail from the container and skid by me. I scrambled to get my feet under me and retrieve them, dignity forgotten. One of the neighbours rushed to my aid. I quickly slipped the teeth into my pocket hoping they weren't broken. Reassuring my rescuers and Ron that the only thing wounded was my pride, I headed to the service wagon.

"Let's get out of here," I gasped as I bubbled with suppressed laughter. Safely turning the corner, Ron and I released our laughter and let it explode, tears streaming down our faces. Ron gleefully asked if that was part of his training.

On another call, Barry and I drove out of the city to a rural area. The house was isolated and difficult to locate in the dark. After speaking to the family and assessing the transfer I returned to the wagon to get the stretcher. The back door wouldn't open. I got the keys from the ignition and tried unlocking it. No luck. I struggled and banged for several minutes. Barry came out of the house.

"What's taking so long?"

"The door won't open."

He took the keys and attempted unsuccessfully to open it. We looked at each other. The family was watching from a window.

"I'll crawl in from the front and tackle it from the inside," I said and walked slowly to front door and disappeared, aware of the spectators in the window.

Once inside, I crawled down the stretcher on my hands and knees and flopped onto my stomach. As I wrestled with the door I heard a tearing sound as the knee of my panty hose caught the zipper. I chuckled. The windows were blacked out so I knew no one could see me and the only one who could hear me was Barry.

"Stop it!" he hissed. I knew he was afraid he would start laughing too. My attempts to open the door failed. In the cramped space I turned around thumping, banging and giggling, and crawled back to the front.

I stared at the dashboard looking for a button that might have something to do with the back door. It wasn't marked, but there was a button and it worked. Wrapping my coat around me to hide the hole, we proceeded with the transfer. Barry and I couldn't look at each other. Being short of sleep made both us inappropriately giggly. At least we weren't irritable. Fatigue didn't have that effect on me until the end of second semester.

I was still enjoying my job. They guys I worked with were, for the most part, terrific. Being on call at night cemented friendships. Because it was hard to go to sleep after a call we'd head for coffee or drive through the city looking at stately old homes or historic buildings. It was interesting cruising the streets in the middle of the night with no traffic. Some areas were best avoided though.

Coming in from an out of town trip in the middle of the night I headed up Yonge Street on my way to the Coroner's office. The traffic was at a standstill, the street at night was lively and bright. While some people looked a little scary, they had their own reality and I wasn't bothered by it. I hadn't locked the car doors.

The removal vehicle attracted a few glances, which I ignored. Suddenly there was a banging on the hood and a group of young men started hollering, surrounding the vehicle. I was terrified and froze for a few seconds. I leaned on the horn scaring them off. I mentioned it to my supervisor when I got back to base. He warned me not to take that route again at night, alone, and to make sure and lock the doors. Good advice, and from then on I was more careful.

Considering the amount of driving one does at a transfer service it was inevitable that the usual problems such as a dead battery or flat tire would occur. During my year at the transfer service I had three of each.

Boosting a battery was easy and help usually readily available – Canadians are used to boosting one another's cars. Flat tires were another matter. My first one happened late on a Sunday night outside a hospital.

As I pulled up to the front door for a quick stop, to scoot in to get the medical certificate, the car lurched and I heard a pop. I approached the security guard, let him know I was on a coroner's call and would be stuck out front for a bit. I radioed base for help and was told someone would be there in about an hour. They asked if I could try to do it myself. One of the guys overheard the conversation on the radio, he was coming off his call and offered to rendezvous with me and assist.

It wasn't the first time I had changed a tire, I just wasn't sure where the spare was. It was under the stretcher in a tray under the floor. I couldn't take the stretcher out of the vehicle at the front door of the hospital so I wrestled with it and the tire underneath for about fifteen minutes. By the time help arrive I had jacked up the car and almost removed the flat. I was filthy and sweaty so I asked my colleague to complete the transfer while I finished the tire. No point in both of us getting dirty.

The second time I was lucky. I was pulling out of base. I just backed up, let my supervisor know, and took another vehicle.

The third time was in the middle of the night in the dead of winter at minus twenty-three degrees Celsius. As I was leaving the highway on an exit ramp the tire blew and I lost control of the van. By the time I got the vehicle under control and safely off to the side of the ramp, I realized I was trapped.

There was a sixty foot embankment less than a foot from my right door and the driver's side opened onto the exit ramp, traffic whizzed by a few feet from that door. I was shaking with fright. This time a tow truck was sent.

One day we were called to a scene to remove a body that had been mutilated by dog who had been locked in with the body for a week. As horrible as it sounds the animal had no choice but to eat part of the remains. The coroner had not even entered the room, he pronounced the death from the doorway. It was our gruesome task to pick what remained.

There was an unusual amount of blood and the officer asked us to check for signs of foul play. He handed me his flashlight and, fighting back nausea, I checked the body for stab wounds or bullet holes. Nothing was evident on cursory examination and we pouched the body for transfer to the coroner's office.

Had we found potential evidence of a crime he would have called the coroner back and the police would have sealed the room. None of the officers wanted to touch the body to check, and I could hardly blame them. It wasn't unusual on a suspect suicide or when something didn't seem right for the police to ask us to roll the body so they could check for signs of foul play.

The coroner has the same powers as a judge, search and seizure. If evidence of a crime is uncovered after the body has been removed to a funeral home, the coroner has the right to come into the funeral home and have the body removed.

One incident in particular, stayed in my mind. A young man had been found dead in his car. There appeared to be no evidence of foul play. The coroner had him transferred to the Coroner's office for autopsy. The pathologist had found nothing amiss. The cause of death was listed as heart attack.

As I assisted the director to prepare him we discussed how sad it was that someone so young had died of a heart problem. She casually remarked about a small hole in his neck. As we continued to discuss it we thought we maybe should bring it to a coroner's attention. From time to time coroners would drop in to sign cremation certificates. The coroner arrived the same day we had discussed the situation, and we asked him to take a look.

"Very interesting," was all he said. Six weeks later he let us know that he had investigated and the cause of death was poisoning. The toxicology reports take about six weeks. The small hole was the entry site – he had been murdered.

Part of our job was to take exhumed remains to the coroner's office to their forensic room if new evidence comes to light. Once, we transferred a casket of a well-known murder case that had occurred years before. We had a police escort from the cemetery and a police officer placed a seal on the door after we brought the casket in the room.

After the forensic pathologist completed the necessary tests, I happened to get the call to return the remains to the cemetery. Once again a police officer broke the seal and my partner and I entered the lab. It felt a little strange to participate in re-casketing the skeletal remains of someone who'd died over a decade ago. We worked quietly and gently. The new evidence led to charges and a suspect was arrested.

One night we were dispatched to a house call outside Toronto to a third-floor walk-up. Neither of us felt like going, we were both drained. At the scene, however, there were three police officers and once we knew help was available we perked up a bit.

The coroner had pronounced the death by phone and ordered the body be brought into an area hospital for autopsy. He had promised to stop by the hospital after the deceased had been transported with the paperwork. We hesitated, reluctant to comply. What if this was a homicide? The police officers concurred. They were as nervous about the removal as we were, but the coroner's word is law.

In the event foul play had occurred what was to stop the coroner from denying that he had requested the removal? That would make the police, and my partner and I, liable. It was obvious that the person was dead, he'd been there for a while and was starting to decompose.

No one had touched the body or entered the room. Gloves had to be worn and the deceased checked for signs of foul play. It is easy to miss something when a body is decomposed and we were not trained in homicide detection, nor was it our responsibility to make that call.

So rather than upset the coroner we did the transfer, only to have the hospital threatened to turn us away because there was no paperwork. They needed the medical certificate of death. All we had was a piece of paper towel with the name of the deceased that a police office had given us. We had the hospital call the coroner who agreed to come in quickly and sign the certificate.

Another time, we were called one evening to a bank where the coroner had pronounced a person who'd died at their desk while working overtime. The body had not been discovered for several days because it was a long weekend. The cleaning staff found the individual slumped over their desk.

It was a cold night. There was a police car out front. We tried the door but it was locked. We blew the horn but no one came to let us in. Shivering we tried the back door. It too was locked. Remembering that my bank card was in my pocket I used it to get into the lobby and warm up. Necessity is the mother of invention. Eventually the police officer saw the vehicle out front and let us in.

When traffic snarls in Toronto it can take hours to go several miles. I worked at the transfer service the day of the Santa Claus parade. After clearing a call north of the city, I was dispatched to a south end central hospital – which meant crossing the parade route.

It took four hours to wind my way down and around. Several times I attempted to cross the parade route but the police on traffic duty would not let me through. I arrived at a major intersection south of the parade in a very bad mood. The transfer service had been asking why it was taking so long. The funeral home had called to complain.

Several officers blocked the west intersection a block from the hospital. I watched as a car tried to sneak past them unsuccessfully.

"For crying out loud," I yelled to no one in particular, no one could hear me. "Enough already!" I slammed the car into park, flung open the door, slammed it behind me, and with my head down, marched over to one of the officers and stated my case.

"Excuse me," I said. "I've been trying to get through this traffic for four hours. I have a body to pick up and I am quickly losing my sanctification. If you don't mind, I would like to get on with it." Yes, I really said that.

I was aware I was eye level with the officer's tie clip. Clearly, I looked and sounded like a bratty little kid. He burst out laughing, which promptly took the steam out of me.

Not to be outdone, he called the sergeant over. With mock seriousness he said, "Sergeant, this lady has a body to pick up. Should we let her through?" The sergeant played along and made me laugh.

As I stopped at the same intersection on the way back from the hospital both officers came to the car to continue teasing me. I couldn't help but appreciate their attitude. It was cold, the traffic was impossible, horns were blowing, drivers were edgy and they still saw the humour in things and managed to cheer up a cranky person.

I had the chance to reciprocate and cheer up an officer several weeks later. I was sent to a city about two hours out of Toronto to pick up a homicide victim and, under police escort, bring the body into the Coroner's office. It meant leaving the city before dawn to meet the police officer by sun up.

When I arrived at the hospital and introduced myself he seemed rather distant. He informed me that he would lead the way until we reached the outskirts of Toronto where I was to take over and lead him to the Coroner's office since he didn't know where to go once he was in the city.

My attempts at small talk fell flat. I did ask him not to drive too quickly because the alignment on my vehicle was off and it was a bit of a struggle staying in my lane. He didn't answer.

Upon reaching the highway the officer set a cruising pace of 130 km. We sailed past traffic and speed traps, the Ontario Provincial Police officers acknowledging the two speeding vehicles with a wave. I was too busy fighting with the car to think about much else except for a few choice words when we got to Toronto.

On the outskirts of Toronto we were finally slowed by traffic and I pulled ahead of him. My hands were stiff from gripping the wheel and fighting with the vehicle. Even at a reasonable speed the car drifted. I made a point to inform my supervisor to pull it off the road.

As we pulled into the coroner's office I got in the first word.

"What are you – the policeman from hell?" I asked. "A hundred and thirty kilometers per hour?"

"I noticed your alignment was off," he said. "Must have been tough to control."

I just looked at him.

"I'm sorry", he said. "I was on this case half the night. I missed breakfast and I wasn't supposed to meet you until later today. At the last minute the sergeant told me to be there early. I didn't mean to take it out on you."

"We both are short of sleep and we both missed breakfast," I responded. "I can fix that, let's get the paperwork done and eat."

After taking care of business, I took him to a restaurant where we talked about our work and parted company in better humour.

Back at school for second term it was fun catching up with my classmates. We knew second term would be a bit more challenging and I knew I would have to cut back and take the occasional weekend off to study.

First day back there was a message for me on the bulletin board to see one of the teachers as soon as possible. Seeking him out he gave me the name and number of a police officer who wanted to speak to me. My first thought was that something had happened in my family. It must have showed on my face because he gave me his office to use.

The officer was calling about a call I had attended, did I remember a homicide at such and such an address? Could I give him the details? He took my statement over the phone, saving a subpoena. He seemed surprised that I remembered so many details.

It wasn't hard, the victim was my age and the details of deaths like that stay with you. He asked me about Humber, what kind of training we received there and mentioned that he thought about funeral service as a career once himself.

There was another notice for me on the board the next day. A funeral home in Toronto had called with an apprenticeship offer. They specifically requested a woman. I had been there several times with the transfer service as a coach driver. I couldn't even remember where the funeral home was let alone the details of my visit there, but they did.

The manager suggested we discuss the apprenticeship offer over dinner. I had hoped to work at home and explained I would not be able to give him an answer right away. Within a few days I had called the funeral homes in my area. There were no positions available in my part of the province. My disappointment was intense. I longed to get back to family, friends and familiar things.

So I called the manager and booked dinner with him. I was wined and dined in high style and presented with an appealing offer. He asked me what my expectations were of my apprenticeship and what they could do it make it work. All he asked of me is that I would not work at the transfer service during my apprenticeship year. The pay was adequate and I agreed to give up that part-time job. It was a generous offer and I accepted. However, I still had to pass second semester.

As my studies intensified, work became increasingly difficult. One evening I lost my ability to lift on a house call. I stared at the stretcher, unable to pick it up. Looking around I saw people who weren't there – I was hallucinating.

A family member stepped in to help. My partner was furious, and rightly so. As we headed out into the cold air I started retching. My supervisor had mixed feelings. How can you work with someone who is going to let you down? We worked with grieving families, it wasn't their job to step in and do mine. I withdrew from being on call, working only (more or less) an eight-hour shift on weekends from there on out.

CHAPTER SEVEN

It Doesn't Have to be That Way

Christmas season at a funeral directors service was a unique experience and I appreciated I had the opportunity to try it – once. Two days before Christmas our shift started at eight a.m. and ended at midnight – sort of – the pagers went home with us. When I wasn't on the road I watched the preparation of a plane crash victim, a task requiring the skill of a talented director whose restorative skills were exceptional. It was meticulous work.

That night I managed an hour of sleep before being jolted awake by the pager. I struggled out of bed, nauseous and shaky. It was snowing heavily and the wind chill factor sat at minus twenty-seven degree Celsius. I was suited and out the door in my usual five minutes, cleaned the ice and snow off the vehicle and drove through the very quiet streets of the city.

At base I switched vehicles, preferring a station wagon as opposed to the van I had taken home. I was going to a nursing home north of the city and the wagon offered better handling on icy roads. I scraped the snow and ice of the wagon, dragged and tugged the stretcher through the snow and checked my equipment and gas. Most night calls require a partner, a nursing home call meant I could work alone. The call was far enough out of town that I would be out of pager and radio range so I let dispatch know when I was leaving.

The directions I had been given were somewhat ambiguous, but I had a good map and figured I shouldn't have too much trouble finding my way. It feels strange driving in a blizzard in the middle of the night surrounded only by howling wind and swirling snow with visibility limited to no more than a few feet during bursts of wind. For some reason the phrase "it was a dark and stormy night" kept repeating in my head.

About an hour later, close to the nursing home, I took a wrong turn and found myself driving down a steep, narrow road. Off to my right when the gusts of snow cleared, I could see a flat area indicating a lake. Realizing my error I turned the car around before I got stuck.

The snow was deep and I accelerated carefully up a little hill. Out of the whiteness there was a car parked, motor running about three metres in front of me. A man stood at the back of the car and he scrambled out of my way. I steered to my left only to have a second car materialize out of the whiteness.

With the road blocked, I had a split second to decide whether to slid straight in or turn and hit the car at an angle. I chose to go straight into the bumper to minimize damage. The impact caused that car to slid about fifty metres down the other side of the hill before it stopped in the snow.

No one was hurt and there was no visible damage to either vehicle. However, there were five men in the two cars who confronted me, all drunk and demanding money. They expected me to pay them and keep quiet. They also refused to produce driver's licences or show insurance. I was furious. Five against one in the middle of nowhere in a blizzard?

I pretended that I was going to radio for police with their licence plate numbers. They didn't know the radio signal was out of range and hampered by the weather conditions. After an ugly confrontation, they moved out of my way. I found the nursing home and completed the transfer, arriving back in Toronto four hours from the time I had departed.

On Christmas Eve morning, I dozed off in a chair at base for a few hours before starting my day shift. There's no good time to lose a loved one but Christmas seems harder. It is a season of giving, which in the face of a loss, changes one's perspective of Christmas for the rest of their lives.

Two of the staff did a house call to pick up a gentleman whose death had been expected, he had a terminal illness. Early Christmas morning as we started our shift, my partner and I were called to the same address, his wife had died in the night, her grief too much to bear.

Late Christmas day I transferred a young man from the hospital to the Coroner's office. The cause of death was alcohol poisoning. Some Christmas party.

Even though it was a bit more hectic than normal with the funeral homes and hospitals on skeleton staff, there was still time made for each of us to sit down to a Christmas dinner – turkey with all the trimmings, provided by the transfer service.

New Year's day was much the same, busy except my partner and I seemed to get all the large bodes, several over 113 kg (250 lbs) and a couple past 136 kg (300 lbs). It was also frustrating dealing with the bureaucratic mix-ups at hospitals which were skeleton staffed again for the holiday.

Our largest body that day was a house call. We were unable to get the deceased through the door on the stretcher. We had no choice but to drag her on a sheet outside to the stretcher on the porch, an extreme last resort measure. Once outside we struggled to try and lift her the six inches to the collapsed stretcher.

I hated every minute as the family stood by watching the less-than-dignified process. Finally, three family members stepped in to assist. I apologized to them for having to use them for such a difficult task. They sobbed as they helped. I felt horrible. It was too much for two tired transfer service personnel, and they were unable to spare anyone else at base.

With Christmas break over and the new semester looming ahead, I felt a bit discouraged. I had not been able to get home to see my family. I took a day off just to sleep. I knew the four months ahead would be some of the most challenging I'd ever face.

Our first day back meant the usual pep talk about the workload, study habits and Board examinations. The class was noticeably smaller. We were given some good news, we'd be changing to a four-day week with Fridays off. Technically Friday was reserved for labs and field trips and we were to be available. Really, it meant more time to work on assignments.

I decided not to work Friday nights. Two days into the new semester we were assigned four essays and two presentations. That meant working Saturday and Sunday only. Nonetheless I found my attitude slipping.

At 6:30 a.m. on a dark, cold and snowy Saturday standing at a bus stop on my way to work to pick up a car for an 8 a.m. flower, I began to seriously question my commitment. Shivering in the dark and cold with tears slipping down my cheeks I indulged myself in a major bout of self-pity.

I had watched classmates return after Christmas tanned and happy from tropical getaways, others rested and contented with the family time and break.

Getting up early to load flowers into an open car and head to a cemetery and reverse the process seemed a futile waste of energy. In the winter, flowers froze within minutes of exposure to the air. At the cemetery the containers blew off the mound, spilling their frozen contents onto the ground. Did anyone notice the flowers? Did I even care?

At that awful moment I didn't. In a way that half hour in the dark was my Waterloo. For after my tears dried I knew I had made the right choice. I recalled the support of the professors and my classmates and the bursary. I still had some of that money, making it possible to continue my education.

I thought of my boss from the funeral home I'd worked at over the summer, he and I had stayed in touch. He was a fabulous cook and he had me over for dinner when we could get together, encouraging me with laughter and support.

I had a great deal of respect and admiration for the staff at the transfer service, they had taken the time to teach what I needed to know to be successful. The bad didn't outweigh the good, the job meant that I was exposed to sadness and grief more than not, making the gentler moments all the richer.

Funeral service isn't about constant praise and recognition. It involves some personal sacrifice, putting other's needs ahead of your own. I had observed the occasional self-centred funeral director, individuals incapable of responding humanely and compassionately to people in acute grief because it might cut into their lunch hour or carry over the end of their shift. I had the misfortune of working with a pathologically self-centred director, who in my opinion, did not deserve a licence.

I watched him as a family came in for their appointment. They were clearly distraught. Thirty seconds into the interview he asked if they had been to the cemetery yet to purchase the plot. Five minutes later he sent them away because they didn't know what services they wanted. He arranged an appointment for them the next day with another director because he didn't want to deal with them, too lazy or indifferent to build a rapport with the family.

When I was doing a reception, he snapped his fingers from across the busy room to get my attention to fetch a coffee. Insensitive and inconsiderate. Any respect I should have had for him was gone, and from then on I ran interference when I could to steer families to another director.

Perhaps he was burnt out. I knew he drank too much, a not uncommon problem among funeral service personnel. He was independently wealthy and could have retired comfortably. At best, he should have left funeral service.

Families seldom complain during their few days at the funeral home. They are immersed in grief. It's after, sometimes months after, they realize that a funeral director may have mistreated or defrauded them. As legislation has improved, the complaint system helps weed out individuals like him

After the flower run, I was dispatched to pick up an accident victim at a small out-of-town hospital. While waiting for the security guard to come with the morgue key, I noticed a police officer standing with a family. He asked me for directions to the morgue, while the family headed for the washroom, clearly distraught. I informed him that the security guard was fetching the key and could help on his return.

My vehicle was parked out front in clear view, so I excused myself and drove around to the morgue so the family would not see a funeral-suited person and a transfer vehicle. I left the stretcher in the car and met the security guard at the door to the morgue. The guard was a high school student. He asked me what to do. He'd never been with a family while they identified their loved one.

The police officer came around the corner. Fortunately he was alone.

"Are you the mother?" he asked.

"No, I'm with a funeral home," I responded.

"I've never done this before," he said, a hint of frustration in his voice. "Isn't there supposed to be someone here? Is the body viewable? I don't want the family to see a mess."

I looked at the two young men who were clearly uncomfortable with their first-time experience.

"I honestly don't know," I replied.

"Would you help me?" the officer requested.

"Sure," I said. "I'll take a look. I can't do my removal in front of your family so I'll be waiting anyway."

The young security guard opened the morgue door and backed away. For a second I thought he might pass out. A grisly mess met us – sheets covered with blood were wrapped around the victims and scattered on the floor. The bodies were intubated, covered with dirt, blood and medical paraphernalia. Their clothing was in shreds. The officer and I looked at each other.

"Shouldn't there be someone here? There's supposed to be someone here isn't there?" he said, voice rising.

"Well…maybe not" I replied. Were you told that a chaplain or nursing supervisor would be meeting you here?

"No."

"Then it looks like it's just us. The doctors' and nurses' jobs are done. I am here for the other victim on behalf of the funeral home."

"My sergeant is going to hear about this," he stated. "This is just not acceptable. Something needs to be done."

I couldn't help but agree. "Not to worry," I said. "We will make it better for the family."

The security guard had recovered from his initial shock and watched as the policeman and I moved the body from a shelf to an empty gurney. I removed the bloody sheets, carefully pulled the intubation and IV's and lines, wiped the blood from his face and brushed his hair over a forehead laceration. I took a clean sheet from my stretcher and covered him.

The two men stood by quietly and respectfully, lost in their own thoughts as I worked to tidy the room, repeating the process with the victim I had come to pick up.

"There," I said. "That's the best I can do. I could get into trouble if someone reports I tampered with a body I wasn't responsible for."

"Why?" asked the policeman, his anger obvious now". "This should have been taken care of before the family came in."

"I agree," I said. "If this were my son or daughter I would not want to see them like that. I think it's a gentle and kind thing to remove the intubation and clean off the blood. This moment and day will be with the family for the rest of their lives."

I suggested we wheel the young man the police officer was there for into the hallway so the family would not have to enter the morgue. He and the security guard went to the lobby to get the family and I went into the morgue to wait while they identified their twenty-something child. It took them five seconds. No chaplain, just a rookie cop and funeral service student who felt it shouldn't have to be that way.

Months later, during my apprenticeship on a transfer to that hospital a security guard mentioned that a policy change was in effect. Only coroner and funeral directors were allowed in the morgue. If family and police officers requested entry for identification purposes the hospital administrator was to be called. Permission was given only after the situation was assessed.

The police officer was true to his word and had followed up as promised.

CHAPTER EIGHT

The Arrangement Interview

The third day into the new semester our newly formed group was pulled for lab. We had yet to go to some of new classes and now we had the pressure of the lab report and all the group meetings related to it.

Six days later I received a call from home, a family crisis necessitated I leave immediately. The shock of the bad news and the long-term effect it would have on our family left me numb and unable to focus. I waited a day to go home, too shaken to drive. I need to process. Emotional shock can affect someone physically and mentally. It was our family's turn.

When I arrived home my husband and I talked for hours. He seemed to feel that the problem we faced would go away, or resolve itself. I didn't agree.

I did some soul searching and wrote a letter to Don Foster, the program co-ordinator, formally notifying him of my decision to withdraw from the program. I notified my lab group so their grade wouldn't suffer because I wasn't pulling my weight, giving them time to complete my section. My priorities were clear, while I didn't want to leave funeral service, my family came first.

A few days later I told my husband I was prepared to give up funeral service and stay home. His response was immediate and volatile.

"Absolutely not!" he yelled. "I haven't gone through the worse year of my life so you can quit!"

I started to cry. I was so wrapped up in school and work that I had forgotten how hard it was for him alone with the kids. We were isolated from each other, our time together limited to a few phone calls a month. I also recognized that the consequences of my decision to enter funeral service had changed the dynamic of our family life – they were moving on without me. I backed away from the discussion to reflect on what he said.

A few days later Mr. Foster called to offer his support. A couple of days later another professor called offering his encouragement too. My husband insisted I return to school, refusing to discuss the matter further. I notified the program office that I would be back and I returned to Toronto to finish what I had started. I was rested and grateful for the friends who'd been there for our family.

Although I had resigned from my lab group because it wasn't fair they should have to carry my workload, my lab partners had refused to accept my resignation. As a team, acting out of compassion, the three of them worked to complete my part. I shared in the grade, another B, but not in the work.

In the school newspaper that semester an article expressed some concern about the cadaver in the Health Sciences Department. Humber College was the only community college in Ontario in which a cadaver is used to teach anatomy to the nursing, ambulance and emergency care, and funeral service students.

The Funeral Service refrigeration unit is secure and the cadaver had been there for years. The author of the article was concerned about the safety of the cadaver and practical jokes that might result. The fact that bodies went in and out of the college almost every day was omitted from the article, the writer clearly unaware of what went one behind those locked doors – a tribute to the respect and discretion shown by the funeral service professors and students at Humber.

Upon my return, I started work again. My partner and I were called to a downtown hotel at a busy intersection. The front desk clerk directed us to an underground parking garage. As we drove down the ramp we realized there wasn't enough clearance. Our attempts to back up on the icy ramp were unsuccessful. A small group of people watched. All we needed was some extra weight in the back but one could hardly ask for volunteers. We were forced to abandon the van, radio for a tow truck and have someone from base deliver a station wagon.

The family did not question our late arrival. They did want questions answered about cremation – did we need clothing? When did they have to sign papers? Where did they have to go? How long would it take?

We told them what we could, suggesting they set up an appointment with the funeral director and reassured them the decisions were theirs. They would be returning to their country after the cremation and could take the cremated remains on the plane with the proper certificates.

Three house calls later my partner and I grew tired. As we were dispatched on our fourth house call I waited by the car while my partner disappeared to the back of the house. He was gone for quite some time and I was considering going to look for him when I heard, “It is her – I don’t believe it!”

A police officer was rounding the corner with a big smile. “Don’t you remember me?”

I shook my head no. He gave me an address. It meant nothing. “Remember that house call you and your friend did? I couldn’t believe they sent two women.”

It was my turn to laugh. “And this woman’s name is Jan.” I said. “Yours?”

“Allan. And I suppose I’ll have to help out again.”

I grinned mischievously. “That would be very gentlemanly of you Allan. But I’m not asking.”

“Huh!” he snorted. Of course he did help and I appreciated it.

The deceased was ten metres down a mossy path in a ravine. The rocks were loose and scrambling up a slippery path carrying a stretcher required the strength of both men. My partner laughed as he told me that Allan had asked about the removal team and subsequently related the story about the two women he had encountered on a house call. When my partner mentioned he was working with a woman, Allan had to see if I was one of the originals. I would have liked to have sat over coffee with Allan, he was quite delightful and it would have been fun to get to know him.

Mid-terms didn't seem as stressful during the second semester. I had been tutoring a couple of students who worked hard, no nonsense this term. Classes continued throughout that week. My Psychology of Grief class presentation was that week as well. We were to give a twenty minute oral presentation expanding our research on an assigned essay topic. My topic was Pastoral Care of the Bereaved.

I grew up going to church and had a healthy respect for clergy believing that "many are called but few are chosen". The ministry was not my choice of a viable career. I seriously doubted I would have been "called" let alone "chosen".

Psychology of Grief was an interesting course. We studied Worden's tasks of grieving, comparing them with Rando's theories and with other theories of grief. We look at suicide and how it affects the survivors. I had experienced several suicides with the transfer service and was aware of the intense pain the family experienced.

I had also observed a funeral, a small private service where the family was deprived of support because they felt there was a stigma attached to suicide. The usual chatter that accompanied visitation was absent from that service. The few visitors who did come, spoke in subdued tones. The family needed support but backed away from it. The funeral director and the clergy need to take the time to work with a family in a situation like that to encourage normal funeral rites.

While researching my paper on pastoral care I noticed a common thread. Minister/priest/clergy spend a great deal of time counselling and helping people face and accept loss. The tone of society does not allow for loss. It is a normal part of life but people prefer to run from the pain, it is easier than turning and facing it. It was not uncommon for a bereaved person to ask, “When will I get over this?” Grief is not something to get over, it is something you go through.

The course encouraged us to look at forms of denial, such as the trend towards immediate disposition. Immediate disposition means removing the body from the place of death and directly to the funeral home to be prepared for cremation, no visitation, no viewing, no service. When a family proceeds with immediate disposition because it was the wish of the deceased, they may short circuit their grief process/journey. There are times of course when it is appropriate.

As funeral directors were we told to observe and listen to the family, and ascertain what effect immediate disposition might have on their grief process. Even if there is no clergy involved we can suggest a memorial service, a short visitation or a graveside service. Some acknowledgment that a life has been lived and a loss has occurred can and, more often than not, take place.

The same is true for stillbirths and even miscarriage. The loss of a baby is powerful. The couple are young and the expectations for a life to come are taken away. The family needs to be supported, not dismissed as if not important. Their grief is negated when one suggests they can have more children and move on with their lives. People do need to move on, but only after they have stopped long enough to grieve. Serious grief can, and probably should last a year or more.

When grief is stuck then a counsellor is needed to help the individual let go and move on.

The psychology course also covered therapeutic communications in response to certain grief-related statements and insinuations. Funeral directors very quickly learn to respond to anger.

Some people deal with grief by verbally attacking the funeral home staff or anyone who will listen. Every now and again there's a family member who likes to 'run the show'. People who express their grief in that manner pose a challenge. They are demanding and assume we are at their beck and call for every little thing. To a point we are. It's our job to serve them and to anticipate their needs, but you meet the occasional family who cannot be satisfied no matter how hard you try.

The transfer service sent me to a funeral home for parking lot duty. The visitations were busy and parking tight. My job was to ask people to back into the spots in order to avoid accidents upon leaving. People are often distracted after visiting a funeral home and pulling out of the spot was safer.

A gentleman with a handicapped sticker tore a strip off me because the handicapped spots were taken. My back hurt, my feet hurt, and I was fed up trying to direct drivers to back into the spots they wanted to pull into. I stood and looked at the angry, sputtering man and did not respond.

It was a beautiful evening. The air was fresh with a breath of spring. It had been a good day, transfers had gone well and I realized I was very content through my fatigue and stiffness. The angry little man had not rattled my cage to the point where it upset me.

As I reflected on his anger it occurred to me he had every right. I was strong and healthy. I had not lost a friend to death. From my place in the parking lot I could see people entering and leaving the funeral home, so I watched for him to come out. As he hobbled past the front door I hurried over to him.

"Can I get your car for you sir?" I asked.

He peered at me through bushy eyebrows and I thought for a second how bright and intelligent his eyes and face were.

"That you can young lady," he said, handing me his keys. "I have no desire to navigate that ravine." The *ravine* was a slope in the lawn, a small ditch. For me it was nothing, for that gentleman it was one more major obstacle to face in his day. I fetched his car and he thanked me.

"I have to go to another funeral home tonight," he said. "Lost two friends this week and one last week." No wonder he was angry.

During second semester the class had the opportunity to go to the coroner's office to observe an autopsy. I was looking forward to watching an autopsy in its entirety. Over the months I had come to know the pathology assistants by name and was looking forward to watching them work. They can make our job easier by the appropriate placement of incisions and tying off blood vessels. The opportunity to watch a pathologist dissect and examine organs was of interest as well.

Over a couple of months, we went to the Coroners Office in small groups. It was a new environment for my classmates who looked around the pathology suite with interest. It was similar to our lab, stainless steel counters and sinks, a table with drainage and medical equipment.

There was another group observing that day, toxicology students from the university. They wore lab coats and looked rather crisp and professional. As the pathology assistant introduced our group to them as funeral service students. I watched their faces closely. A few smiled politely, a couple of foreheads wrinkled in what appeared to be derision. They stood well back from the action at the table. We didn't. The pathologist invited both groups closer and our group, curious and interested, complied.

The processes and procedures were explained and each organ identified. The deceased was a suicide and was not decomposed. There was no odor. The pathologist was happy to answer our questions and was a good teacher.

Shortly after the abdominal cavity was opened there was a flutter of activity across the room. One of the university students bit the dust. His friends didn't quite know what to do. No one moved to assist him so I went over, loosened his collar and tie and rolled him into the recovery position. As he started coming around the pathology assistant, who I had chatted with many times in my job, came over, winked at me and assisted the poor guy out of the lab.

Autopsies are observed by many health care groups and related professions such as police, ambulance, lab technicians. A few minutes later some of the white-coated students started slipping out the door, stating they wanted to check on their friend. Within five minutes they had all gone to check on him. They didn't return.

The pathologist showed us how he examined the gross anatomy of each organ, while the pathology assistant showed us how he took samples and specimens. It was a fascinating experience, one that our entire class appreciated.

On April Fool's day one of our classmates pulled a stunt that was talked about for years after, reminiscent of Inspector Lessard's experience in the movie Police Academy.

We were in Theory class, a three-hour session on chemicals, buffer pairs, modifiers etc. Important, but boring. During the break a classmate of ours slipped into the lectern. A few of us saw her crawl in and she swore us to secrecy.

When John Finn took his place and started class she waited a few minutes, then tugged his pant leg. Most of the class were unaware of her presence. John certainly was. For a few seconds he looked like a cadaver, a shocked expression on his face, frozen in position. He then erupted into howls of laughter and as our triumphant classmate emerged, our shrieks and screams of laughter exploded. There was just way too much merriment to continue class and we were dismissed. The professors checked under the lectern each time they entered class for the remainder of the semester.

As part of our training in the last semester, we were assigned a role-playing arrangement interview. Initially we formed groups of four and used first-call sheets as checklists.

Very few students goofed off during those practice sessions. It was one of the most important skills a funeral director learns.

The checklist covered introduction to the family, the atmosphere set by the director, how the director responded to questions and volunteered information, how much concern he or she showed, how flexible, attention to information requiring registration, etc. Our group was hard on each other, assigning low marks for our first attempt.

Three of us would enact the role of family, sometimes we were walk-in's (no appointment), other times we made appointments, giving the "director" time to get organized.

We were so caught up in our role playing that sometimes the tears were real. We did a scenario where a baby had died of SIDS (Sudden Infant Death Syndrome). As the funeral director asked the family who had walked in "how can I help you" the mother blurted "how the hell can you help me? My child just died!" and she started to cry, for real. We were a bit taken aback.

The funeral director bravely continued the interview. After we had evaluated the interview, the student who had been the mother explained the exact same situation had occurred when she was on duty at the funeral home she worked at.

We put ourselves through several arrangement interviews, each in preparation for the final interview in which a professor from the college, a support staff person, or an outside funeral director would role-play a situation in which we would be graded. We had no information, we walked into the assignment cold.

Sometimes appointments were arranged and posted on the board, other times a student would suddenly be pulled from class. We were to dress appropriately. For several weeks I was on edge, eager to address the challenge. It was the culmination of all the months of preparation to become a director, off limits to all us until that day.

I checked the board hourly, my name wasn't there. My group made up business cards for 'Humber Memorial Chapel' and arranged for each other to serve as support staff, making the introduction and fetching coffee.

Several weeks passed. Finals were a week away. Most of the interviews had been completed. From my conversations with my classmates about their arrangement interviews I was convinced of one thing – the purpose of the interviews was to encourage us and to send us into our apprenticeship with some confidence.

In between classes our final week the program secretary stopped me in the hall. "Can you do your interview now?" she asked.

"Certainly," I replied cheerfully, displaying a confidence I didn't feel.

She handed me an arrangement folder and I told her I would be right in. I retrieved my business card from my locker, found one of my group, and had her follow me into the office. A tall gray-haired gentleman stood there. We were introduced. I looked him in the eye and gave him a firm handshake and greeting. I offered coffee, which he accepted and I sent my classmate to the cafeteria (that part was real). We were seated and I asked how I could help.

The first twenty minutes were spent listening. He repeatedly asked me what to do, what did I think? I gave him options and explained that the decision was his. He wanted cremation. At that time Ontario law stated that forty-eight hours must pass from the time of death until cremation.

As the interview progressed I relaxed a bit. Even though I was concentrating on my body language and was practicing attentive listening skills, I was aware of some tension. As we finished our coffee and wound down the interview, I handed him my business card.

"OK," he said, all business and taking over. "Let's evaluate this situation." He identified himself as the Program Co-ordinator of one of the business departments at the college. The role playing was real, the situation had occurred in his family several years before. He like the coffee and the card, a business-like touch. He commended me on my listening skills and assigned a grade of 99% - typical of what my classmates had reported.

While it was an important skill it was assigned a low-weight factor in our overall grade. I felt it was one of the most valuable experiences in my training.

Just before final examinations, the applicants for the Funeral Service Education Program for September came in for testing. They looked scared and awkward. Some of us took the time to ask them where they were from and did our best to put them at ease.

During their testing we peeked through the window of the classroom door and reminisced about our testing day. One of the professors told us there were three hundred and forty applicants for the one hundred and twenty-five positions. Our chances had been better.

The final few days of the semester were spent catching up, which for me meant Restorative Art. Over the course of the semester we were required to produce two wax heads, one from measurements and the other from a picture. We also had to apply cosmetics using four different types of mortuary cosmetics. Each assignment was graded.

The wax heads required hours of work for those of us who were not artistic. We took advantage of the extra lab hours, crowding into the space to complete our task. A photography student who was also trying to finish a semester assignment on “A Day in the Life of Humber” was given permission to photograph us. It was a strange sight, dismembered wax and plastic heads on the tables and counters. He was introduced by our instructor who glibly said to him “if you want to get ‘a head’, come to this class.” We laughed. The photography student didn’t, nor did he stay very long. Not everyone is comfortable with what a funeral director does.

Our final day of school was a field trip to a casket company, several funeral homes, and the Foster mausoleum. The bus trip was fun, we were like grade-school students singing and joking. Someone took a great photo of John Finn glaring at the group of songbirds from the front of the bus.

One of the funeral homes provided us with homemade cookies and treats. The casket manufacturing process was explained and types of caskets identified. I couldn’t help but noticed what a different group my classmates were from months ago. They appeared more professional and confident, less ragged and insecure. I was going to miss school. It had been one of the best years of my life.

My apprenticeship was to start in a few weeks. The company had paid for my Board registration, my suit had been fitted, and I was looking forward to my internship year.

The night before finals, I got a sudden sore throat. "Just nerves," I told myself and tried to concentrate on my books. The sore throat, however, was not nerves. The morning of my first exam I ran a slight fever. Not too bad, but Tuesday's exam was Theory, my nemesis.

My fever had climbed and I ached all over, finding it hard to concentrate from the discomfort. We had three hundred questions to complete in two hours, questions such as:

> ***extravasation is:***
>
> a. passage of dissolved substances into the blood
>
> b. passage of dissolved substances out of the blood
>
> c. decreased by increased capillary permeability
>
> d. increased by decreased capillary permeability,
>
> e. responses 2 and 4

I did my best, finished my exams feverish and ill.

At the end of the week John called me into his office.

"How did you find the Theory exam?" he asked. I'm sure he knew from my demeanor during exams that I had been sick.

"I came out of that room wondering what the hell happened," I responded.

"Board exam format," he replied. "Maybe it went better than you thought," he said kindly.

I shook my head. He would not have called me into his office if things had gone well. He then proceeded to tell me why he "kept after me" in class over the semester. At the time I thought it was because I sat at the front.

"You were the colour of the wall," he said. "I knew that some nights you didn't get to bed. I kept after you to keep you awake."

"I thanked him, grateful for the support he and the professors had given. It was time to start a new chapter.

That evening only one formality remained, a dinner and dance. My voice had been claimed by laryngitis and tonsillitis. Although I was achy and tired, my husband and family had come up for the party and I wasn't going to miss it.

We presented phoney awards such as: To the student most likely to host his own TV show "Fun with Funerals" – given to our class clown. We had door prizes donated by funeral homes and suppliers.

As my husband and I stood outside to get away from the noise, John Finn came out. I introduced my husband to him and John commended him on his support of me during the year.

Turning to me, John said, "You will do well. You will be a good funeral director." And he swept me up in a big hug. My eyes brimmed with tears.

"Far cry from our first meeting, huh?" I said, and we laughed together.

A week at home helped shed the fatigue and flu, and I went back to Toronto ready to start my apprenticeship. My marks arrived several weeks later. I managed 65% on my Theory exam. The Board examination pass was 65% and it would be written in fourteen months. It was clear John had given me a strong warning not to let up.

You were allowed three attempts if you failed a section of the Boards. The year before us seventeen students had failed a section of their Board examinations. Marks at Humber seemed harsh but the reality was that the marks usually fell within three percent of the Board's marks.

CHAPTER NINE

The Undertakers are Here

The funeral home I apprenticed at required us to wear our funeral suit all the time. This identified the directors to people coming in, and gave us a uniform, professional appearance. It eliminated the expense of suits and dresses.

During quiet time all the staff was responsible for upkeep, which included cleaning, dusting, washing floors, and windows, lawn and garden care and cars. I was informed by my supervisor that my main area of responsibility for the first few months would be the cleanliness and stocking of the preparation room. I was also in charge of lawns and gardens. When I wasn't occupied I was to make sure the prep room was disinfected and ready for the next call.

As the apprentice, I was would be doing most of the embalming while on duty. For the most part I worked a forty-hour week. At least that's how it was supposed to work over the six-week schedule. Week one was thirty-three hours, week two fifty-four hours, etc. I was paid for overtime. There was no night call, the transfer service took calls after 9:00 p.m.

The first week on the job we received five calls in one day, more than our chapel could accommodate. Four of us worked until the wee hours of the morning prepping and setting up. Not one person complained. We communicated information correctly and thoroughly, and the tasks were completed on time.

During visitation one of the families squealed with delight over the flowers. They ignored the open casket and spent most of their time in the lounge with their visitors. Other families ignored the lounge and spent their time at the casket with their visitors. It was interesting to observe different reactions by different families.

The prep room became my "office" and I started moving from theory to practical. One of the cases I prepared the first week required some creativity. The deceased had jaundice. If the incorrect embalming fluid is used, the bilirubin converts to biliverdin, turning the body green, then black. (Bilirubin is found in the bile, it breaks down old red blood cells.) The family chose a peach outfit and a peach-lined casket. The result after embalming and before masking with cosmetics was hideous, a peach and yellow clash. I went into my restorative art notes at home, and back at work the next day using an opaque cosmetic I applied a pink base with brown highlights and red overtones. The result was a dramatic improvement and the family was pleased.

One of the advantages of working in Toronto for my apprenticeship was the exposure to multicultural groups and different mourning and burial rites. The funeral homes were able to accommodate all faiths and cultures. Hindus, for example, have many sects and each sect has variables in burial customs.

We had a hibachi which we set in a sandbox in the chapel so they could burn leaves and other symbolic items during the service. At the cemetery, the family would place a sheet on the ground five times as the pallbearers carried the casket to the grave and five times the casket would be placed on the sheet. The graveside service could be lengthy, sometimes lasting over an hour.

Buddhist funerals were very detailed as well, fresh white flowers were important and they were replaced daily on the Buddhist stand. Roses were not sent by friends, they were considered to be an insult and if we found an occasional rose in a bouquet we would pull it.

Some cultures are reticent in their grief, others, such as Italians were more demonstrative, outwardly expressing their grief by wailing and weeping. I came to view their method of grieving as healthier than my strict protestant upbringing, where silence surrounded death. Tears are a sign that a person has the courage to face the pain and release the emotions. Suppressed grief is like a beach ball pushed beneath the surface of the water. It will resurface over and over. Grief is work and grief's work must be done.

The funeral home did not have a funeral coach, it was shared with other funeral homes. The family limo was also shared. My favourite job on a funeral was coach driver. It is dignified, you don't get dirty and you follow the lead car. Since the funeral coach came with a driver that left me to do the flower runs. That meant loading the flower tray into the van (heavy and awkward), followed by the flowers, (heavy and messy) into the van, racing ahead of the procession to the cemetery and once there, locating the grave, and with arms full and as fast as possible, racing back and forth from van to grave placing the flowers (neatly). Then back to the van and to the cemetery gate to turn around and await the procession. It was then my job to lead the procession to the grave.

I was terrified I would take a wrong turn and end up winding endlessly through the cemetery with the procession behind me. I actually dreamt about it.

Often there wasn't enough time to plan a route into the grave site. If the procession was large it had to be routed to maximize parking so other funerals coming in would not be blocked. It was a nerve wracking job, more than once the procession was a minute or two behind because they often had a police escort to the cemetery. I would leave the funeral home about the same time as the procession because the flowers couldn't be loaded until the chapel was clear of people and I had to contend with traffic and stop lights.

One very hot and humid summer day on a large church funeral I went ahead of the procession to place the church flowers, leaving the rest in my van. I assisted the coach driver wheeling the casket up the aisle, and back down as the service ended. It was then my task to line up the cars after the service, ensuring their lights were on. As the last few cars cleared I hurried to the van. I could see the lead car pulling out behind me. The cemetery was over 50 km away. I had written the directions, which were a bit complicated, on a napkin which I pilfered from the staff room, it was on the seat beside me. Because the van was full of flowers I had tossed a pair of comfortable shoes into the van. I shed my heels and put on my flats, changing them at a stop light.

The napkin directions were accurate and I found the cemetery. I ran into the cemetery office with the burial permit and asked directions to the grave. My tires squealed on the hot pavement as I took off as quickly as I could from the office.

The vault company truck was parked near the grave set-up. I jumped out, threw my jacket on the grass and started running with the flowers. The heat and humidity was horrid and after my first trip I was sweating. By my second run I was panting. There were no trees and the grave was well-off the road. The two men from the vault company watched me from the comfort of their air-conditioned cab.

About ten trips later I was soaked with sweat, it was dripping off the end of my nose. Tires squealing again I headed back to the front gate of the cemetery. I glanced up and down the highway looking for the procession, changed back into my heels, wheeled the van around and yanked down the mirror to check my makeup.

I gasped in horror. I have white hair, it was streaked and dotted with orange. My face, neck and ears were orange. I had tangled with some tiger lilies. Their pollen comes off the stamens easily but it doesn't brush off or wash off well. It has to be scrubbed off. I looked hideous. My jacket was dusty from reaching in and out of the van to grab flowers. The sleeves on my blouse and the front of my blouse was orange.

"What am I going to do?" I said out loud. My heart was pounding. I picked up the only thing I could find, the napkin with the directions and started scrubbing my face. Mix ink with sweat and pollen and you get the picture, I was blue and orange. Now I was in full panic mode. I raced for the cemetery office washroom.

The light was burned out and I couldn't see what I was doing. I soaked some paper towels and racing back to the van – I could see the procession coming down the road.

As I drove to the graveside I had trouble focussing on my directions, I was too busy scrubbing my face. Because the cemetery had no trees I used the vault company van as a beacon and managed to get the procession to the grave without getting turned around. I did my best to keep my head down, I had to take the end of the casket with the pallbearers on the sides and the coach driver at the other end.

My orange streaked hair caught the sunlight. The lead director walked up and surveyed me from head to toe. I kept my head down so he couldn't see my face.

"Nice hair," he said dryly.

"I had a fight with some tiger lilies."

"Obviously."

I helped place the casket and retreated behind the van. Cemeteries are usually quiet peaceful places. I was learning fast there was nothing peaceful about flower runs.

Flower runs are fraught with mishaps. Short people carrying two baskets of flowers in their arms have their vision obscured. More than one director has fallen into a grave because of flowers. I remember it happening to one of the directors. All I could see when he went down were the tops of the gladioluses waving in the breeze. On windy days baskets will tumble merrily through the cemetery usually followed by a funeral director or assistant.

Back at the funeral home my boss told me about a funeral procession he'd taken out the year before. The student who'd been sent ahead with the flowers was nowhere to be seen as they approached the cemetery. The director led the procession to the grave after stopping at the office to get directions. Still no van. As he approached the grave he saw the van but no student.

Upon closer inspection he could see the top of his head at ground level and baskets of flowers flying through the air as he pitched them up from the grave. The wind kept blowing them back. He didn't see the procession coming and the family was not impressed. If there is that much work and responsibility with flower runs, I was in no hurry to lead a procession.

When I did lead my first procession my boss didn't tell me until the last minute, so I wouldn't get nervous. The procession consisted of two cars, a coach and the lead car. My boss sat in the back seat of the lead car and the minister was in the front with me. As I accompanied the minister to the car to open the door for him I let him know it was my first procession. I figured he had a right to know he was dealing with a novice.

I drove slowly, but not slow enough. My boss kept telling me to slow down. The lead car driver needs to have an unobstructed view of the procession from their left mirror. The coach driver is supposed to know that and stay in line. He was oblivious. When I moved slightly left, so did he.

The coach driver is also supposed to maintain a car-length distance behind the lead car. If you are starting into an intersection it is the coach driver's responsibility to hang back a bit to let oncoming traffic see that a funeral procession is coming through. My coach driver didn't know that. He puttered behind me, leaving a gap of three or four car lengths, just enough for someone *not* in the procession to cut in. That happens frequently in a busy city, people are in a hurry and don't have the same respect for funerals as they did years ago.

As a coach driver with the transfer service, I loved to cut off people who tried to cut into a procession. It's a big vehicle and most cars would not want to run into it. I have known coach drivers to get out of the coach during a procession and yell at drivers who were being rude by trying to cut through the procession.

A frontend loader came out of a construction site in front of me. "Oh shit!" I exclaimed. Immediately I realized what I had in the presence of the minister, and my cheeks flushed with embarrassment. What a hypocrite I was, after telling others not to swear.

It's not easy switching lanes in a procession. The coach and limo drivers are usually alert to potential problems and should move as one unit with the lead car. That is not always possible in heavy traffic. You are responsible (not liable) for the safety of people in the procession. Once they leave the service at a church or funeral home they are distracted, often driving through stop lights and signs in order to stay in procession. That is why in a large busy city, a police escort is recommended.

I signalled a lane change and cut over. My coach driver didn't. He slowed and stopped for the frontend loader. It took him a few seconds to realize the front loader wasn't going to move for him, so he signalled and eventually switched lanes. Traffic meant he and the procession were way behind me. By the time I got to the cemetery I was so rattled I forgot to get the flowers out of the trunk.

As I stood listening to the minister to finish the committal service I looked down into the grave. It was double depth. When I leaned over the do the committal sand I envisioned falling down into the twelve-foot hole. I did remember to pull some roses from the casket spray for the family.

Back at the funeral home my boss sat down and explained what I had done wrong. I had driven too fast, cornered too quickly, forgot to take the flowers out of the trunk, should have been more alert to the frontend loader ahead, etc. etc. He concluded with, "And you never use profanity in front of a minister."

I was embarrassed. As a general rule, I tried not to use profanity in front of anyone. I think my hours and hours alone in the transfer vehicles had been my downfall. It wasn't unusual for me to curse when I was alone in a vehicle where no one could hear me. I made sure it never happened again.

One of my classmates was apprenticing in a partner funeral home, we often worked together on funerals as drivers, or paired up for transfers. Together we were sent to one of the most prestigious nursing homes in the city. It was elaborate and ornate, resembling some of the older funeral homes in the city. There was no staff on the first floor, one of the residents let us in and informed us the nurse was on the second floor.

It was very quiet there too and we approached the nursing station. The nursing assistant took one look us, and hollered, “Marsha, the undertakers are here.” ‘Marsha’ was down the hall, showed us where to go, unfazed by her co-workers yelling. We held our laughter until we reached the van.

Several weeks into my apprenticeship as I was transferring from one of the hospitals, I picked up the medical certificate and slipped it into my pocket. As I approached the body to check the ID I noticed a red tag. That indicates that universal precautions should be exercised, the person died of an infectious disease. They were, in effect, biohazardous.

I pulled the medical certificate from my pocket and checked the cause of death. The disease was on the list of reportables, that is, the

Medical Officer of health must be notified as to the cause of death. Sometimes the MOH will order immediate cremation. In this case the MOH had allowed the release.

Ideally two people would affect the transfer in this situation. The disease listed was more virulent than I was comfortable with. The morgue attendant stepped in, handing me an extra pair of gloves.

“Be careful with this one,” he said. “This virus can kill you two weeks. The pathologist said to tell you that if you are pregnant or have been sick lately, don’t work on it.” He helped me move the body. Back at the funeral home I got one of my co-workers to assist.

When I explained the cause of death to my boss he looked at me blankly. Funeral directors are required to attend post-graduate training every five years, but in spite of that the disease meant nothing to him.

“Frankly”, I said, “I would sooner work with hep C.”

“You don’t have to prep if you don’t want to,” he replied. We can notify the family and have a hermetically sealed casket or send the body to the transfer service for embalming. You are the most recently trained and know about this disease so I will defer to you."

"I can do it," I replied. "I worked and observed infectious embalming at the transfer service. All I ask is that the prep room be off limits to staff for the next five hours, No phone calls and no interruptions please."

I sat down for lunch and mentally reviewed universal precaution procedures. The funeral home was well equipped with body suit, goggles, masks, hair and shoe covers. I didn't like to double-glove - it reduced tactile skills, but it wasn't an option. All unnecessary equipment was removed from the prep room. I laid out everything I would need, double-checked it and confined my workspace. Concurrent disinfection was an important part of the procedure and I made sure I complied.

It took longer to ensure the disinfection of the deceased and the room that it did to embalm. The biohazardous material was secured and the prep room disinfected thoroughly. As students, we would grumble about lab, a lot of what we did seemed unnecessary, such as washing the cupboard doors for the third time. What we were being taught was the best way to do something and we learned three or four ways to do it. The safest method of working on human remains was always stressed. All the cleaning and disinfecting was training for a day like today and exposing students to a variety of situations and techniques meant we were better prepared. I didn't mind working alone for those hours, in fact I rather enjoyed it. It wasn't as stressful as taking out a procession.

When an individual dies of a disease such as tuberculosis, spores are released. With the rise of drug-resistant TB, for example, even a tiny drop of blood on the floor, when it dries out can release spores, sending them airborne if someone brushes them with their shoe.

One of the strangest transfers I did was a radioactive body. When I arrived at the admitting department to pick up the death certificate, the clerk told me the head of nuclear medicine needed to speak with me.

The doctor explained the deceased had been given a radioactive isotope injection and died in the process of having a nuclear scan, a new procedure in those days. That meant the deceased was radioactive and we should limit our exposure to one hour. It was very considerate of the doctor to let us know, chances are we could have been exposed for a least six hours without that information.

As Thanksgiving approached I headed home for the long weekend, eager to visit my family. That weekend I had a horrific nightmare. I dreamt I was standing beside a casket, reaching down to the bottom to retrieve a bolt I needed to close it. The body was shrouded with the casket lining. A cat came into the room, covered with blood. Her tail was puffy and she was angry. As she swished her tail she splattered blood all over the walls.

"Oh," I said, "I have to get you to the vet's, you're hurt" and I pulled my arm out of the casket to help her. The cat was hissing and spitting. As I approached her she collapsed. Suddenly seven men entered the room. Not one word was spoken. They just stood there sinisterly watching me. Something was wrong.

"Get out," I said.

They didn't move.

"Get out! I yelled. "Get out! Get out!"

The next thing I knew my husband was calling my name and shaking me. I could hear and feel myself yelling "Get out!" The dog was whining. I had wakened everyone. The dream didn't make sense to me other than as a warning that I needed to ease up a bit. I had no social life, no form of relaxation. I had hoped second year would be easier, however, stress is cumulative.

I was starting to show the stress at work as well. Coming down the aisle during a church service, wheeling the casket to the coach, I crashed it into a pew.

I was supposed to lead a procession to the grave at the cemetery and didn't make on time, unable to get all the flowers I was placing unloaded quickly enough. Little things, but a good warning. If you put too many bales of hay on a camel's back it breaks. Removing the bales one by one does not change the fact that the camel's back is still broken. Those incidents were a forewarning of a situation that nearly cost me my apprenticeship.

One evening on a transfer, I went to the admitting department to pick up the death certificate. I was known by sight now. There was no one at the desk. I sighed impatiently. I could see the medical certificate on top of the chart. Tired of waiting, I picked up the medical certificate, signed the book, and left the transfer slip that let the admitting clerk know what funeral home I was from. I asked the information desk to page the morgue attendant who opened the morgue and I completed the transfer.

I had no idea of the trouble ahead. The admitting clerk called the funeral home and complained. I should have waited. How dare I rifle through patient's charts, etc.

Hindsight is a perfect science. I was tired and in no mood to be accused of rifling through a chart. Nor did I think I should have had to wait as long as I did before I took the medical certificate. So, stupidly and without justification I drove back to the hospital and confronted her. While I made an effort to be pleasant and tried to apologize, I made a remark I would regret for the rest of my life. When she pushed back I told her it was one of the worst admitting departments in the city, effectively accusing her of being the worst admitting clerk in the city.

It was several days later before the impact of my remark reached me. The admitting supervisor called my manager and banned me from the hospital. My manager was furious and by the time he was finished with me I was shaking. The disgrace nearly cost me my job. I had only myself to blame, it was a stupid thing to do.

This situation gave me cause to reflect on my choices after graduation, if anyone would hire me or if I graduated. I felt I would be happier in a small town funeral home. I had been sending out applications but had been unable to secure an interview. Funeral service is a close-knit community and being banned from the hospital meant a lot of people heard about the incident. I knew it could be a while before I secured a position.

CHAPTER TEN

You Have to Start Somewhere

After the incident at the admitting department I made a point of getting out and exploring on my days off. The area I lived had parks and gardens and I found that I enjoyed puttering through the mall on rainy days window shopping. I was learning to push my job out of my mind.

One quiet evening while watching TV, the senior director called. He wanted to know if I had seen the wedding band for the gentleman I had dressed and casketed earlier that day. I rhymed off the list I could recall – watch, tie clip, lapel and glasses. I did not recall the wedding band the director on duty with me had listed as part of the personal effects. I drove to the funeral home and started searching the biohazard box and garbage. Nothing. The family had requested that the jewellery be returned prior to the service the next morning.

Keeping track of personal effects is a must. The funeral home is liable for the cost should an item be misplaced, lost or stolen. The director logs personal effects with the family present and they initial a receipt. The ring was listed.

The director and I checked the pockets of the jacket the deceased was wearing. As a last resort we lifted him up. The ring was lying underneath the body. In hindsight I suspect the senior director was teaching all of us a lesson. He had noticed that the director who had taken the jewellery did not pass on the list and should have. I, in turn, should have checked the file in the office for the list. It was a relief to find the ring and all the staff was reminded that no matter how busy we were, to ensure all the details were covered.

As we'd searched for the ring that night, the senior director told me about a situation that had occurred in one of the other funeral homes we partnered with. In between visitations a man entered and looked at the names on the board. When questioned by an approaching funeral director he mentioned a name and headed for the suite. Sensing that something wasn't quite right the director followed discreetly and watched.

He observed the man removing the deceased's ring. The director yelled at him to stop. The man bolted from the suite, knocking the director to the floor. The receptionist called the police who found the director sitting on the man down the street from the funeral home. The director mentioned later that he was so angry he did not stop to think he might have been in danger.

A funeral is public and when something goes wrong it can negate all that went right. One of the biggest concerns a funeral director has is to post-embalming purge – the evacuation of fluids from the mouth or nose. Often this is linked to embalming failure, the funeral director did not do his or her job properly. However, there are situations where it cannot be helped.

If a family member throws themselves on the body in the casket the risk of purge is increased. A body that has not been embalmed poses a very high risk of purging. Purging is a natural consequence of decomposition, it occurs much faster when there is no embalming.

A couple of times during the early part of my apprenticeship, the body I had just prepared purged as we lifted it into the casket, soiling pillows and lining. My supervisor was not impressed. During visitation I would keep an eye on the bodies I had prepared. It is understandably traumatizing for families when purging occurs.

Over time my technique improved. Once in a while a body cannot be salvaged, the decomposition process is too advanced when the body arrives at the funeral home. One gentleman had been dead for a week before he was discovered. Although we worked half the night, he could not be saved. Tissue gas was present and nothing we could do would halt the spread of the bacteria.

The family was informed of the problem and advised to close the casket. They refused. The body was grotesquely bloated, malodorous and black. Nonetheless they insisted on seeing him and leaving the casket open. If the family insists and they are well-informed it is not the funeral director's right to refuse their request.

The family did not seem too upset by the sight. They did have a number of questions about his appearance, which the director tried to deflect. Finally, he came to get me.

He informed me that since I had recently graduated I could give them a technical explanation on decomposition. I was puzzled by his request, but he was my boss and I went into the suite. They asked what tissue gas was. I launched into a technical explanation of Cl. Perfringens, how it had an affinity for soil, how it caused gangrene in WWI and how, once inside the host it produces an exotoxin that sped decomposition, etc. I suggested it might not be a good idea to touch him.

While I was answering their questions I could hear the bubbling and crackles of the tissue gas marching through the body. One of them asked me how to clean the stains on the floor where he had purged at his home. Chances are the flooring would need replacing, but they could try a solution of hypochlorite to clean the surface, disinfect and remove the odor.

By this time I was sure I would have grossed them out, not my intention at all but they kept asking more and more questions, so I understood why my boss wanted me to give them the technical answers. It just fueled their curiosity.

They asked about breathing the air in the apartment where he died, then expanded the question to ask if prolonged exposure to a body in that condition would make them sick. I hesitated before answering, then suggested they ask their doctor, since I wasn't qualified to answer that question.

As a student it was my job to do indigent burials, and I made the most of the situation. I hated that people died alone and destitute. I never could, and never would, just plunk the casket on the lowering device at graveside and leave the cemetery staff to bury anyone. It was disrespectful.

Nearby cemetery workers waiting for me to leave so they could complete the burial would be recruited to act as mourners while I read a short burial service. I would give the committal sander to one of the workers as ask them to act a funeral director. Undoubtedly, they had watched hundreds of services over the years with minimal to no participation. I would read the service, the "mourners" standing respectfully with heads bowed. When I gave the signal for "earth to earth" the cemetery worker would perform the time-honoured tradition with dignity and respect.

Initially, the staff at the funeral home teased me but didn't push it too far. Ceremony is important and I believed it was necessary even when there was no one other than staff to share in it.

Some of the most moving ceremonies were Royal Canadian Mounted Police funerals. Those ceremonies were rich in colour and tradition. A special pillow was sent from Ottawa for the cap and medals. A flag draped the casket. Traditionally, only the sword, cap and medals were placed on the flag on the casket so the family flowers were placed in front of the casket and off to the side. An honour guard of two red-suited Mounties stood at each end during visitation. We had coffee and snacks for them upstairs in the break room. They were such gentlemen and so good looking in their red serge that we girls on staff were slightly giddy.

The day of the funeral a full honour guard of eight assembled in the suite to prepare to proceed up the aisle of the chapel. Another director and I transferred the casket from the bier to the church truck. The combined weight of the deceased and casket was over 400 lbs. As I lifted my end my face turned crimson from the exertion and I expelled my breath with a whoosh as the casket was lowered onto the church truck. The other director laughed and made fun of me.

The casket had to be juggled until it was evenly placed and he made sure it wasn't just so he could continue to tease, watching my face colour with the effort. Finally, one of the Mounties who had been watching couldn't take anymore.

"Ma'am," he said politely, "there are eight strong men standing here. One of us should be helping." I looked at them. The shortest Mountie was over six feet tall and they were gorgeous in their red serge uniforms. It was my turn to chuckle, the joke the director had tried to pull on me backfired on him. I watched them wheel the casket to the front of the chapel and observed the service which was performed with great dignity and respect.

A few months after the RCMP funeral we had a police service which was held at a church. I was assigned to parking lot duty, a redundant job since the police were doing it. I suspect my boss allowed me to come so I could watch. Hundreds of officers were in attendance from all across the country. About an hour before the service was to start, a car rear-ended another vehicle on the street outside the church, pushing it onto the church lawn.

"Watch this," one of the young constables on parking lot duty said to me. Within twenty minutes the cars from the accident had been moved out of sight. With the police chiefs and commissioners and politicians expected, the officer in charge of parking made sure there were no foul-ups.

The young constable snorted. "Any other time it would take an hour to get a policeman at the scene, let alone clear it."

I nodded in agreement.

As the cortege came down the street, squad cars appeared at intersections halting traffic in all directions. Police officers lined the street and saluted as the procession passed. The dignity and pomp gave me a lump in my throat as they buried one of their own.

Meanwhile, every few weeks our second-year assignments we due. A letter arrived at the funeral home for me. Thinking it was my marks I abstractly tore it open. I scanned the letter, not quite taking it in. Several words caught my attention, one of which was "congratulations". My heart skipped a beat. I had won an award – the award that my friend and I had discussed in first year, the one given to the student who showed compassion and concern to their fellow students by helping them with personal and academic endeavours.

Tears spilled from my eyes, I felt honoured. It wasn't until a few weeks later that I found out that a monetary award was presented with it. Of all the experiences during my two years at Humber, winning that award was the most significant. My friend had received an academic award and many of my classmates had as well.

The first six months of my apprenticeship were to be spent in the preparation room. For many of us as apprentices, arranging funerals was in the future. Occasionally, however, when there were only two us in the funeral home, the director and I, several families could come in at once.

One evening while the director was with a family, another group came in to pre-arrange a funeral for a pending death. I explained that I was a student and that the director on duty would be not be available for another hour or so. Would they like to make an appointment?

"Well, can't you do it?" they asked. "After all, you have to start somewhere."

I knew I could probably get the process started and the director on duty would ensure the family's needs were met, so we sat down to discuss their wishes.

I took the information needed for the file. When the director was free he could have taken over but instead he showed me how to complete the contract and checked the details to ensure everything was in order. The family had been composed and pragmatic. As they left, they thanked me for the help.

Several days later I was washing the whitewall tires on the service car outside the garage when I saw them come into the parking lot. They emerged from their car carrying clothing. I dropped what I was doing and went over to them.

"I guess we have to sign some papers," one of them said. "Can you get him from the hospital for us?"

"Oh, I'm so sorry," I exclaimed. "When did your dad die?"

"This morning," was the reply. "Maybe we should have called."

"Not at all. Come in, and I'll get the director for you."

Taking them into the funeral home I introduced them to the director.

"Can't you see us?" they asked. The director agreed it would be acceptable if he sat in on part of the arrangements while we completed the documentation and organized the service.

Some directors just do not like to abdicate responsibility or delegate their responsibility to students. If an error is made it could be their licence on the line. He agreed to join us in a few minutes and I offered coffee.

One of the daughters said she would go to the lounge with me. As we proceeded to the lounge she burst into tears and wrapped her arms around me, sobbing on my shoulder. My boss came around the corner, watched for a few seconds and withdrew.

When she regained her composure and rejoined the family he told me to go ahead without him. He felt that family was comfortable with me and he did not wish to intrude. I appreciated his sensitivity and made sure he was aware of all the details before they left. He reviewed the paperwork with me to ensure compliance and offered his advice on the funeral. Although I was to be off the day of the funeral I would, of course, come in to assist. It felt good to be involved from start to finish and to be able to complete the services to the family.

A similar situation occurred a few weeks later. We had nine new calls that day. In a case like that we recruit students and directors from partner funeral homes who might be free. All calls were covered but one. Seven men walked in, no appointment, to discuss prices. I took them to the lounge, the only available free space and notified the director.

"Just do what you can," he said, obviously frazzled. "Why can't people book ahead?"

I understood that from our perspective booking ahead helped us, but from the perspective of family, booking ahead meant nothing. Since they were price shopping it seemed likely they would not stay to make arrangements. We were most likely their first stop.

In some cultures women do not come in to arrange a funeral, nor do they get involved. This group of men were Muslim. They made their displeasure clear when I explained the director was busy with another family. They did not wish to deal with me, a student and a female.

Sensing their reluctance and slight hostility, even though I could not understand their language, I chose to make the first item of business an offer of coffee. I handed them the price list. They were not exactly forthcoming with information and I gave them time to acclimatize, withdrawing while they discussed the price list.

When I returned after coffee they asked about the size of the suites, so I gave them a tour. The suites were in use but they could gauge size from the doorway. With eight calls and three suites we were limited as to the room available should they decided to stay, which I deemed unlikely. Their only option, in light of the number of people they expected for visitation, was to use the chapel – over which they expressed considerable displeasure.

That left me with one option, to recommend another funeral home. I explained that funeral home had rooms that were adequate in size, and that the prices were comparable. Surprised by my recommendation they asked me why I would send them to the competition.

"It is about your needs, what you want," I explained. "Obviously the chapel is not want you want, the other funeral home has the space you need." I offered to call ahead and make an appointment for them.

They walked away from me to discuss it. The spokesperson turned to me.

"We will stay," he announced. "You are honest, and we like that." Since the deceased was to be shipped overseas, I called the transfer service to get the cost of the repatriation. I explained that they would need a sealer and/or a hermetically sealed casket and the Health Department documentation stating that the deceased was free of infectious disease and what documents would have to be obtained from the consulate. The men requested that I ensure that twenty-six seats were book on the same flight. The transfer service would take care of that part for us.

We spent a long time in the selection room where I explained how a hermetically sealed casket worked. The key (basically an Allen wrench) would be taped securely to the outside of the casket prior to shipment and as an added measure of precaution they would be given one to take with them on the plane. If they chose to use a wooden casket with a sealer, then they would have to take a Robertson screwdriver with them since most countries outside North America do not use Robertson screws.

When they arrived in their country they wanted to have a service with the casket opened. I knew that culturally they would be touching the deceased often and they wanted him to feel natural.

With the time period involved (about two weeks) and the fact the body had to be thoroughly disinfected, the fluids we used to embalm would be strong with the unfortunate end result that the body would not feel natural, it would be firm and rigid. Preservation by embalming is indefinite and depends on a multitude of variables. Some bodies stay preserved for years.

I pussyfooted around the terminology, trying not to get too technical but aware they needed the information and understanding. Clearly, I knew if someone mentioned "firm and rigid" for someone I loved who was being embalmed I wouldn't be pleased. They asked me to explain the embalming process in detail and asked that someone with more experience do it. I didn't mention I had completed a few hundred cases, it was a moot point. I did explain the body would be prepared at the transfer service since they were the experts in repatriation worldwide.

When a family asked about embalming I did not refuse to answer. Some directors felt it shouldn't be discussed. Keeping in mind how one would feel if it were my family member being discussed, I did my best to explained embalming in terms of disinfection and preservation.

The senior director poked his head in several times to check on things. He was rushed and a tad irritable, but he didn't show it in front of families. He suggested I muddle through as things appeared to be OK so far and later, over dinner (we had missed lunch and breaks) we would review the situation.

Four and a half hours after entering the funeral home, the group of men left with instructions to bring clothing and the passport, and to call if they had any questions.

I was very surprised they allowed me to work with them, my past experience with their culture meant my immediate dismissal and replacement with a male director. Their situation presented a few new challenges which we overcame. There was work to do, hours on their call not to mention the other eight. It had been quite a day.

Friends and acquaintances would ask me how I could do my job, especially baby funerals. It's never easy but age didn't seem to affect me as much as the individuals who were left behind did.

I found it challenging to work with widows or widowers who lost their spouse of fifty or so years. One dear little lady was a classic example. She could barely get around the funeral home with her walker. Whenever we did anything for her she was gracious and appreciative.

On the day of the service she met with her minister for prayer prior to entering the chapel. As she passed me she smiled a brave little smile, two tears trickled down her cheeks. I held her gaze for a second but had to turn away, a lump in my throat and tears burning my eyes.

When I started arranging funerals I noticed that most people would break down during the arrangement interview. When I mentioned this to one of the directors he scoffed, stating that in his years of service that situation had only happened to him once or twice and that I being too emotional.

At first I was taken aback by his remarks thinking I was doing something wrong. But as I thought it through I felt the opposite, that I was doing something right. In a therapeutic relationship, such as the one between a funeral director and a client, trust is important. I couldn't just go into the arrangement interview with the attitude that this was a business transaction. It is, of course, but it's also more than that. A funeral director is a grief helper. If taking the time to talk to the family about their brother, sister, mother, or father made them cry, then so be it.

Grief starts with the realization that a death has occurred. Making funeral arrangements is one of the steps in the grief process and the first step after the death. A family is going to respond to anyone with a sincere, open, honest and caring attitude, male or female. People in pain are acutely sensitive to indifference and effective communication is a learned skill. All of us, male or female, use our personality to some degree as helpers when someone needs us.

The basis of a helping relationship is the establishment of trust. The funeral director must listen to the family's emotional needs. Arranging a funeral is more than just an exchange of information, it's an exchange of emotion and meaning.

The most effective tool the funeral director can use during the arrangement interview is to listen actively and attentively, giving their full attention to the family. Attentive listening involves non-verbal as well as verbal skill. Two thirds of communication is non-verbal.

The most awkward part of the arrangement interview for me was the selection of the casket. It made me feel like a used car salesman. Services and professional services such as administration, organization, documentation, preparation, facilities use, vehicles and support staff had to be covered, that part didn't make me feel uncomfortable when price was discussed. The service charges were calculated to cover the overhead.

The average funeral home in Ontario handles about one hundred and fifty calls a year. Seventy-five percent of all funerals in Ontario take place in ten percent of the funeral homes. This meant that for most funeral homes in the province there was no profit in the service charges. A funeral home must be maintained and staffed twenty-four hours a day. Therefore the profit for the seventy-five percent came from the sale of caskets and urns. Disbursements such as cemetery charges, cremation fees and press notices are monies paid out in cost on behalf of the family.

I just hated selling caskets. That is where the funeral home I was apprenticing at made most of its revenue. I had felt no pressure from management to sell or upsell caskets, so I'm not sure what caused my discomfort.

I would closely watch other directors in the selection room hoping to learn from them. When a funeral director shows a family to the selection room he or she usually takes the family to the lowest priced unit. Cremation containers (cardboard or particleboard) may not be on display, depending on the funeral home. If a family has chosen immediate cremation they do not need to see caskets or containers. Under the Act a funeral home must carry two wooden, two cloth and two metal caskets at minimum.

The casket usually has a card listing the price of the unit on top. On the back of the card a funeral home may list their service charges and the casket price added together. Provincial sales tax and goods and services taxes and the disbursements are extra. Ideally once the director has shown the three basic units, they will withdraw from the room to give the family some time to make a selection. For many families, selection of a casket is the most difficult part of arranging a funeral. If the casket selection is based on emotion, an inappropriate expensive choice could be made. This is unfortunate, because most funeral directors have awareness at this point of what the family can afford and the family should never feel pressured to spend money they don't have or could use elsewhere.

Casket manufacturers have seminars to teach directors the features of their units, rather like car salesmen. I just couldn't get past the *selling* part and would volunteer information in the selection room only when the family asked for it.

Every funeral home in Ontario is required to supply a price list upon request, at no charge, to anyone who asks.

Ideally the choice of a funeral home, all things being equal, should be based on the services the funeral director provinces. In a tight market the service charges and casket prices are close.

The family should ask themselves if the funeral director is meeting their needs, are they attentive and interested in what they want? Are your wishes being honoured or does the funeral director try to change them? Is the funeral home environment comfortable? Has the funeral director answered your questions and volunteered information?

When a family is not happy, the first step would be to approach the funeral director and manager. If that fails there is a complaint process via the Board of Funeral Services. I have known of funeral directors who have had their licences revoked, suspended or restricted. Charges against a funeral home or director could include violation of the Act, breach of confidentiality, charging excessive fees, accepting commission without disclosure, charging interest on the account without notifying the consumer, failing to carry out the terms of a contract, allowing staff to act as a licensed director, falsifying documents, refusing services to a person without recommending a reasonable alternative, embalming without permission, impairment by drugs or alcohol on duty, misconduct or unprofessional conduct.

I knew a funeral director who lost his licence for a year for swearing at a family member. The first part of the complaint process goes to the Complaints Committee and Discipline Committee composed of lay members and funeral directors appointed by the Lt. Governor in Council.

If that isn't successful the next step in the complaint process is Tribunal. At the time of this writing, no funeral director who had a case brought against them before the Commercial Registration Appeal Tribunal under the Ministry of Consumer and Commercial Relations has won. The Tribunal has always ruled in family's favour.

The message is clear, it is critical for a funeral director to keep the lines of communication open and be honest, even when something goes wrong.

CHAPTER ELEVEN
Through a Child's Eyes

Children are always be welcome in a funeral home. To a child the fear is often worse than the reality of death. I clearly remember my mother dying when I was four, I did not attend her funeral. In my mind she just disappeared, it was fifty years later when I visited her gravesite. It was as if I had to see for myself.

Many times parents would ask our advice as to whether or not their child should go to visitation or attend the funeral. I turn the question around and ask the parents how they feel about it. As parents we tend to draw on our own experiences as children. It was not uncommon to hear responses such as "I was seven when my grandfather died. I wasn't allowed to go to the funeral home" or "my parents didn't talk about it. I had to stay home". They were left with a sense of unfinished business that carried into adulthood. Invariably they think their child should go but don't know how to approach the subject.

If the child is young we give them a colouring book, Saying Goodbye by John Saynor, a minister and licensed funeral director. We had pamphlets for the parents on the subject of children and death, and encouraged the parents to read the brochure and go through the colouring book with their child before bringing them in.

An honest open approach is important. Phrases such as "grandma is sleeping" only add to their confusion and the child may not want to go to sleep for fear they will not wake up. We suggest the child write a letter, draw a picture, or leave a memento in the casket, whatever makes them comfortable.

Children find their own level of acceptance, asking questions, inspecting the casket, then often running off to explore the funeral home. It is a good idea to have another adult stay with them if they are very young, so the parents can greet visitors without interruption and the funeral home staff is not chasing them all evening. Left to their own devices a child may intrude on another family's grief. Reverence and respect can be taught, but that job is up to the parent, not the funeral home staff.

Several kids I worked with were memorable. One four year old girl was attending the visitation of her uncle. She was quite chatty and liked the office, banging on the typewriter keys, rearranging the donation cards, then off to the lounge to rearrange it. We did our best to entertain her but we were busy and she wanted to be busy too. At one point, she stopped working on the picture we had encouraged her to draw and stated, “That man in the living room has no legs.”

It took a few seconds for me to clue in. She had gone into the suite, looked at her uncle and saw what we all see, just the top part of him. If it had been possible I would have taken her into the room and raised the foot panel of the casket to show her that he still had his legs, but the suite was full of visitors. The director told her that his legs were covered up, just like he had a blanket over them.

“Oh, she said, her face showing her bewilderment. Then, “Why are his eyes closed? Is he sleeping?”

“No,” the director told her. “He’s not sleeping, he’s dead.”

“I know all about that.” She lowered her voice. “He got a cold and went to sleep.” She paused for a few seconds. “Why did he die?” The conversation seemed to be going in circles.

I asked her if she had been to a funeral before. “No,” she said importantly. “This is my first.”

"Would you like to see the chapel where the service will be?" I asked.

Nodding, she slid off the chair and took my outstretched hand. In the chapel's muted lighting and silence I explained as carefully and simply as possible what was going to happen the next day.

"And," I added, "you will sit up front with Mom and Dad, that's a very important seat. I know it's hard, but you have to try to be quiet for a little bit. That will help Mummy. Do you think you can do that?"

She nodded solemnly.

As we left the chapel she dropped my hand and ran to the suite. A few minutes later she emerged with her grandfather in tow. Pulling him into the chapel she dropped her voice and told him that the minister was going to talk and her uncle would be there in his box and that she had to be very, very quiet.

True to her word she was quiet and still during the service.

Another little fellow came in to see his grandmother. I had pre-arranged the funeral and found the family to be practical and devoted to each other. They prepared the children ahead of time. He came through the front door of the funeral home looking very grown up in his suit and bow tie. I greet him and his mom and dad, and took them to the suite. He eyes never left me as we talked. I withdrew and peeked around the door to watch as he placed the "letter" he had written in the casket.

It was a private visitation with the service in the suite so it was about an hour when I saw him again.

He marched up to me, tugged my jacket and said, "Am I going to see my grandmother again?" His tone of voice and solemn little face threw me for a second. He looked so vulnerable. I sank into a chair, making us eye to eye. He stared intently at me as I struggled to find an answer. Two of the staff looked on, glad it wasn't them.

"Uh – what did Mommy say?" I asked. I knew the service had been led by a minister but I couldn't say, "Yes, your grandma is in heaven, you will see her someday." That would have been imposing my value system, and heaven was an abstract concept for a five-year-old.

He shrugged. I told him to ask his Mom and he ran off to ask her. I looked at my colleagues.

"You handled that one badly," said the other director, but he smiled as he said it. It was the little guy's intensity that caught us off guard. The director did not offer any suggestions. I think he was stumped too.

A young fellow around ten came in with his dad for a visitation. The father made him sit in the foyer. The boy threw himself into the chair, crossed his arms and legs and muttered angrily. It didn't take an expert in body language to get the drift of what was wrong. He argued with his dad but the father was adamant. The son waited until his dad was in the suite, then tried to sneak around the corner. It didn't work, he was out in a jiffy.

Since I had a few minutes I wandered over to see what he had to say. I opened up the conversation with, "Don't like funeral homes huh?"

"It's not that," the boy said, sticking out his chest. "I can handle dead people. Dad won't let me go in."

We chatted some more. I learned that the deceased was a co-worker of his father's.

"He died of a stomach ache in his sleep," the boy told me. "I have a stomach ache just like his."

In his not so subtle way he revealed his fear. I asked him if he wanted to tour the funeral home. Of course, we didn't go to the prep room but I did answer all his questions about dead people. He seemed to like the selection room the best, admiring all the caskets with comments like "wow – look at this one" and "is that ever neat." When we went back to the hall he was smiling and laughing and eager to share his new knowledge with his dad.

Second year was moving by quickly. It meant starting to review for Board exams and booking a room at Humber residences for the two-week consolidation period prior to Boards. I was being given more responsibility as an apprentice under the watchful eye of my supervisor.

If the flower runs I did could be fraught with mishaps, then I quickly learned the cemetery was as well. It was always fun to listen to veteran funeral directors swap stories of pallbearers being fished out of a grave. More than once I have watched a funeral director leap into action to prevent a casket from falling because elderly or weak pallbearers could not get the casket lifted over the lowering device on the grave.

Usually the casket is not lowered completely with the family present. Large cemeteries have their staff move in as soon as the mourners have cleared. They do not like it when funeral directors activate the lowering device. Smaller cemeteries have no such rule.

One fine spring day, five of our staff stayed behind to lower a casket into the grave at a small church cemetery. The family and friends had proceeded into the church for a reception. There was no device, the casket would be lowered by two webbed straps. It had been sitting on boards above the grave for the service.

The four men were to raise the casket while I pulled out the boards. The plan was for them to slowly lower the casket down. The men at the front of the casket were having a little trouble lifting the casket high enough for me to get all the boards out.

The director gave the OK to pull the final board and with a tug that required all my strength I pulled it free. With a sickening thud, the casket slammed to the bottom of the grave. The lid of the casket sprang open. All five us started in fascinated horror into the grave. It took a few seconds for the director to recover.

Glancing furtively around to make sure no one was watching, he jumped down into the grave and closed the lid. We silently helped him out. As he dusted himself off the men started arguing angrily as to who was at fault. One of them started to laugh. We turned and stared at him. Another one joined in the laughter and a chain reaction of laughing was triggered. We howled merrily, gasping and wiping the tears from our eyes. The laughter was not meant to be disrespectful. It was borne of relief – immense relief that no one was hurt and no one else had witnessed the incident.

Cremation in Ontario occurred thirty-five to fifty percent of the time, depending on the location. Northern crematoriums were scarce, a funeral home could be several hundred kilomters away from a crematorium. In the cities there could be several.

In spite of the commonality of this method of final disposition, I had yet to watch the crematorium staff load the retort (cremation chamber). Family members may attend and if they wish, push the button to fire the retort.

When I first started arranging funerals it was obvious I would not be put with a family requiring a full traditional funeral. You start small, arranging a service with no viewing, or with immediate dispositions. There are still a number of details to keep track of, and to a funeral service student it is challenging being responsible for keeping them straight. Over several days a director may be managing more than one funeral.

One day I answered a call from a family about pre-arranging a funeral on the advice of their minister. They asked about prices but were reluctant to make an appointment to set up tentative details. They phoned a number of times with questions prior to the death.

When the death occurred they again were reluctant to proceed with funeral arrangements, putting it off for a few days. Eventually arriving with their minister, they made it clear that there was to be no body or urn present. They did not want visitation but at the prodding of the minister agreed to have a memorial service with no funeral director there.

They insisted the burial of the cremated remains take place immediately after the memorial service. I informed them that our services at the graveside would not be necessary, that a family member or friend could lower the urn. At this point they hesitated. They did not want a funeral director present but they did not want to handle the urn.

Several times during this challenging arrangement interview, one or more of the family would break down and ask to be left alone. I would quietly withdraw and wait for permission to return to continue. They were struggling with what we all face in grief, the desire to face the death and the wish to push away the pain.

The minister, who was not the most endearing individual, listened and gave advice. He felt strongly that the cremated remains be present at the memorial service. I supported the family's wish about not having a minister or urn at their memorial service. He was annoyed and, in my opinion, getting annoying.

"We'll see about that," was his curt reply.

The first order of business was the cremation. I met one of the relatives at the crematorium. The retort was cooling down and we had a chance to talk. The in-law was from an ethnic background that encouraged viewing and touching and he found it disturbing that there was no visitation.

When we entered the crematorium he viewed the cardboard container with disbelief. The crematorium staff and I backed off to give him time to say a final goodbye. He cried quietly for a few minutes and stood aside to watch the staff load the container. He was invited to fire the retort, and he stepped forward to push the button. As we left he remarked on how moving the experience had been. It was my first time watching the process and it had all the solemnity of a burial.

Back at the funeral home one of the directors told me a touching story about a client whom he had

served some years before. He was an elderly gentleman who used to sit on a bench in the park across from the funeral home when the weather was nice. One day he came into the funeral home to prearrange funerals for himself and his wife. She had been ill for some time and he was her caregiver.
Upon her death he took her cremated remains home.

Several years later, the coroner's office called the funeral home to come pick him up at his home. There was no family. He died alone. The arrangement file had a notation that the cremated remains of his wife were to accompany him to the funeral home and be placed in his casket.

The junior director did not know the man and started scouting the house for the cremated remains. The senior director knew exactly where to look. Opening the refrigerator door he pulled out the lettuce crisper and took out an urn. The urn was covered with travel stickers. Since this gentleman's wife had not been well, they had been unable to travel together. After her death they travelled the world.

The day of the memorial service I prepared the urn and paperwork. The family had requested that I proceed to the cemetery about half an hour before the start of the service and wait by the grave. Ten minutes before I was to leave the funeral home the phone rang and an angry voice at the other end of the line demanded that I bring the urn to the church immediately. The minister hung up. There was no discussion. Thinking the family had changed their minds I scrambled to collect what I needed.

As I was leaving, my boss warned me to check with the family, suspecting the minister was dishonouring the family's wishes. The other director warned me not to let the minster push me around.

At the church I locked the cremated remains in the car and went inside.

"Well? Where's the urn?" the minister asked.

"In the car," I replied. "Has the family arrived?" The parking lot was full, it was going to be a large service.

"No," he stated. "Get the urn."

My heart started to pound. I hated confrontation.

"I have to speak with the family outside," I said. "They specifically requested that no funeral service personnel be present at the church."

"Wait in my office," said the minister as he pushed me toward the door. When it shut behind me I knew I had been outsmarted. The second the family arrived the minister seated them and let me out.

"Get the urn, go around to the back of the sanctuary. Bring it up the aisle and place it on the altar. And when the service is over, walk back up the aisle, pick up the urn and lead the procession out."

I was starting to get angry and I was a bit frightened. This man was showing total disregard for the wishes of the family. In a voice that shook with a combination of insecurity and anger I replied, "I can't do that. I *must* speak to the family."

"Who is running this funeral?" he said, his anger matching mine. "This is my church, you will do as I say."

I lost my courage. It flashed through my head that it was God's house, but I kept my snarky thoughts to myself.

"My manager will have to hear about this," I replied.

"Damn right he will!" he stated and he pushed me out the door. I retrieved the urn and handed it to the assistant minister at the back of the sanctuary, leaving him to proceed up the aisle with the urn, and with tears of anger and frustration, headed for my car, driving straight back to the funeral home.

Seeking out the manager I reported the sequence of events and the conversation the minister and I had. The manager told me to get back to the cemetery and ask the family to come to the funeral home after the reception. I didn't ask why, I complied, happy to be alone to muddle over the situation.

I waited by the graveside. After the service the minister led the procession out of the church, carrying the urn. He saw me, moved ahead of the group of people and handed me the urn.

"Place it," he said curtly. The air was thick with tension. I complied rather than make a scene. I walked away, sought out one of the family members, asked them to stop by the funeral home later, returned to the car and drove off.

Upon my return to the funeral home the manager met me and took me to the staff room. He closed the door. Suddenly I had the feeling something was not right.

"You made two mistakes today," he said. He was definitely not smiling and I started to feel sick. I honestly thought I had handled the situation well.

"You never question a minister. When he gives you an order, you follow it to the letter. It is his church, and yes, he *is* running the funeral. I will be going over to the church to apologize for your behaviour. We depend on the clergy for referrals and you jeopardized that. You never do anything to upset them, ever.

"Secondly," he added, "you did your family a great disservice."

At that point I had no idea what he meant by that comment. He went on to explain that when the minister made the remark "we will see about that", even if it had been muttered under his breath, it was my responsibility to take the family aside and let them know, tactfully, that they should speak to the minister themselves.

"It is not your job to fight the family's battles for them. When they come in you will sit down with them and apologize for your actions. In the meantime, I have to clear things up with the minister." He stood up to leave. "And I'm not happy about it."

As he left the room I headed for the washroom where I released the pent-up emotions. I sobbed until there were no tears left. I was confused. My supervisor had told me to check with the family, I had tried. The other director told me not to let the minister push me around. The minister did push me around, literally. It felt as if I had been bullied and he won. I was devastated by this unexpected turn of events, I honestly believed I had done my best to honour the family's wishes, and to be told I had let them down was devastating.

Downstairs both directors who had given me advice prior to the service would not look at me. They were aware that the discussion upstairs had not been amicable. I had not implicated them in any way, the manager did not know about their input. I was determined to keep it that way, even though I could have told the manager. I was angry and having trouble accepting full responsibility for the situation. They could tell I had been crying.

I took a deep breath. "I really blew it," I said and I told them what had transpired upstairs. I did not let on that I had done my best to act on their advice and orders or that I felt they were a little bit responsible for the outcome. They had always treated me with respect and been more than helpful. I made it my problem and I owned it.

When the manager returned from his visit with the minister he did not acknowledge me or speak to me. I overhead him discussing the situation with my supervisor and he was obviously still angry. I retreated downstairs to clean, staying out of everyone's way.

When the family came in later, the manager took them into the arrangement office and came looking for me. He asked me if I knew what to say. I simply nodded, anxious to get it over with and not trusting myself to speak.

As I entered the room the family looked concerned. At first I thought the manager might have talked to them but I realized they had not been in the building long enough.

"I have something to tell you," I said. "I am afraid I have let you down." My voice broke and tears welled. I explained in full what had happened and how I tangled with the minister. I ended with, "I will be apologizing to him as well."

"Is that all?" said one of the family members. "My God, we thought something was seriously wrong, like we buried the wrong urn or something."

"This is serious," I said. "I should never have tried to fight your battle. I will be apologizing to the minister as well."

"Oh, for heaven's sake, it's no big deal," one of them said. They were obviously relieved nothing had gone amiss with the inurnment.

"You did a fine job and we appreciate your efforts," said another. "Is your manager upset? He didn't seem very happy." I just nodded.

"Well," said the spokesperson. "Where is he? We will straighten this out."

"No, but thank you." I replied. "It has been a difficult day for you. I appreciate your understanding. Again, please accept my sincerest apology."

They rose to leave, gave me a hug and left in good spirits. I closed the door to the arrangement office and called the minister. He was not very receptive. I didn't make excuses or defend myself. I was still angry and my apology was not heartfelt. I found my supervisor and asked for the rest of my shift off. Yes, was all he was prepared to say, and yes was all I wanted to hear.

Several days later a box of chocolates arrived for me at the funeral home. I had been keeping a low profile, seeking every opportunity to hide from the staff. The manager presented the chocolates to me with a flourish in the staff room and everyone laughed when I opened the card.

My admirer?

The minister. Fences were mended and he and I got along quite well after that.

A lesson had been learned – practice what you preach – facilitator, not functionary.

CHAPTER TWELVE

The Board Exams

Reactions to a death on the part of a relative are as different as the individuals themselves ranging from complete indifference to extreme, debilitating grief.

A busy executive came in to make arrangements for his father. He came alone, the arrangement interview was brief and businesslike. The first evening of visitation we had to keep his visitors waiting for quite some time in the lounge because he was late. He breezed into the funeral home, announcing that he was a very busy man.

The director ushered him into the suite to give him some quiet time alone. He gave the suite a cursory glance, grunted his approval and informed the staff to let his visitors in. During visitation he stayed at the back of the room, greeting people jovially. As soon as the stream of visitors slowed down he left, leaving one of his employees to greet his visitors. The next day he again sent one of his staff to cover for him. He showed up briefly, wearing jeans and a sweatshirt. He left three minutes later. He did attend the entire funeral seemingly more out of a sense of duty than desire. If he was grieving, he had buried it, feigning indifference, avoiding the pain.

Some families become very involved. One family I was serving were late for their appointment to make the arrangements, but they arrived attired in suits and behaving formally. As I led them to the arrangement office I asked one of the sons if I could take the clothing for him. He clutched it to him and politely informed me that it was fine.

My supervisor came in to check to see how things were going, he asked the same question and got the same answer. The arrangement interview lasted three hours, the family questioned everything on the contract and made it quite clear as to what they expected. I dutifully recorded their wishes. The last item of business was to turn over the clothing.

When they arrived for visitation they kept their visitors waiting while I adjusted the flowers, moving pieces several inches right or left on their behalf. They were quite happy with the way the deceased looked and once they had spent some time with him, asked that the casket be closed.

Each time new flowers arrived it was the same scenario all over again, they had to be shuffled and readjusted. If a petal or a leaf fell to the floor in the process we were warned to be more careful. Every now and again they would come out and ask me to open the casket for certain visitors. This required two staff members because of the type of casket selected. Only two of us were on duty, it meant the phones were unattended while we complied with their wishes, being extra careful not to jostle the large casket spray.

On the day of the funeral one of the sons took over. He set the agenda, reinstructed the pallbearers and questioned every move the staff made. He supervised the loading of the flowers in the service van and made sure I knew where each arrangement was to be placed at the church and cemetery. His inability to relax and let the staff do their jobs meant the service started late.

The clergyman was waiting when we arrived at the church. Some ministers and priests operate on a tight schedule and will cut the service short if they are inconvenienced. No spiritual benefit or comfort for the people who attend if the minister is rushed.

As we left the church I was on the back end of the casket, which meant I instructed the family to follow me down the aisle. We try to wheel in and out with some dignity, moving evenly and slowly. Someone kept stepping on my heels and crowding me. It was the son, anxious to get to the back so he could join the pallbearers. I ignored him and held the casket firmly so it wouldn't surge forward when he pushed.

The coach driver at the front of the casket sensed the problem and also assisted by pushing back. As we reached the exit one of the family members fainted. I left my post immediately to assist. People were trying to stand the person up and I was having trouble making myself heard. I finally made sure the individual was lying down. I was unable to move them into the recovery position because people were pushing and crowding.

The son moved into the vacated spot at the casket and started drumming his fingers impatiently. He was scowling. When he felt he had waiting enough he instructed the coach driver to proceed to the coach. The pallbearers stepped in. This time, the minister stopped him and curtly told the son to wait until everyone was ready. Because of the crowd it took a while for the family member who had fainted to recover enough to be assisted to the limo.

I gave the pallbearers their instructions and assumed my position again only to be physically shoved aside at the coach door. I didn't see him coming. When the coach is being loaded the pallbearers are instructed to place the casket on the second set of rollers and step back. The person on the end, (me) is then responsible for pushing the casket into the coach.

On that second set of rollers the casket is not at fulcrum point, it is in a precarious position and can fall. I stumbled and the casket teetered. The coach driver was alert and quickly grabbed me. With his help I steadied myself and completed my task. It was a close call.

At the cemetery, we waited for all the cars to park. The procession was long and it took a bit of time for people to walk to the graveside from their vehicles. Again the son headed for the back of the coach. In his impatience he opened the coach door and proceeded to give the pallbearers the order to remove the casket. The coach driver stepped in and blocked the casket and told the pallbearers to wait for the director's instructions. The son was furious.

Once I returned to the coach and the clergyman gave his nod, I instructed the pallbearers to turn away from the coach. They all complied, except the son, who was trying to tug the casket out of the coach. We waited patiently until he recognized he wasn't on the same page as the rest of us. At the graveside he stood beside the clergyman, making it difficult for the lead director to take his place. His job beside the clergyperson is to hold anything they need held, such as a prayer book or incense and then step in to do the committal sand at the end of the service.

After I returned the family to the limo the driver said his piece. "Looks like he's planning to become a funeral director", he said dryly.

As annoying as this gentleman was, I recognized some people have to exercise their need to control. Perhaps by attempting to control the funeral he felt he had control of his emotions. When there was a male director on duty the odd compliment would come my way from a pallbearer or male family member such as "you did a reasonable job for a woman". There is no point being offended, some men just need to be in charge and grief may bring out that trait. The main thing is to serve them to the best of my ability.

Some people become very dependent during the period of the funeral. A professional woman in her late thirties, very attractive and well-presented, exhibited her grief openly, sobbing uncontrollably during the arrangement interview.

She was unable to make decisions except to express her wishes as to how she wanted the deceased to look. On her first visitation her siblings had quite a time coaxing her into the room. Once she approached the casket, supported by her family, she fussed over the deceased's clothing and hair, making tiny adjustments.

As visitation progressed, she regressed. Her voice became more and more like a little girl and her dependency grew to the point of asking someone to unwrap a candy for her. The family rallied around her and complied with her every wish. At the church, she stood numbly while I removed her scarf and coat. It was like undressing a small child.

Some people are prone to fainting and we keep oxygen handy, as they may faint more than once. One lady who had collapsed for the third time that day gave me a few tense moments. I could not feel a radial or carotid pulse. Her respiration was slow and shallow. I rolled onto her back and checked again, hoping I didn't have to start CPR. As the oxygen took affect her pulse fluttered beneath my fingers. As I put the unit away I had to sit down until my legs felt stronger.

The oxygen was also helpful when one of the visitors had a severe asthma attack. Her lips and fingertips were blue and her breathing laboured as she struggled to get air into her lungs. The stress of coming into the funeral home had triggered the attack. She usually carried her inhaler and oxygen with her but had left them at home, thinking she was going to be all right.

One of the saddest cases of grief was a gentleman who lost his wife. He was well-educated, dignified and polite and seemed quite calm on the surface. Four days after his wife's burial I walked into the prep room. He was on the table, a bullet hole in his head indicating the cause of death. The family was in shock. He had been unable to deal with his grief.

Another tough situation was the funeral of two small children. It was a media circus, reporters called the funeral home and followed the family's every move. The service was private and no information was given out by us. There was no press notice. Nonetheless they media pursued them. It was difficult for us to make it possible for the family have some privacy. Media was camped on the edge of the property and we couldn't be sure they were not sending someone in on the pretext of visiting another family.

We closed off half of the funeral home and let only staff through. I had helped prepare both children and worked with the parents to dress and casket them. The other directors and I did not hide our tears as we worked with this family. It was very depressing.

As my apprenticeship year drew to a close I could not wait for it to end. It was difficult for me to be a student. My age, personality and background rebelled against the submissiveness of the role. The day I turned in my key for the funeral home should have been a sad one but it wasn't, although I knew I would miss most of the people on staff. I had learned a great deal over the twelve months, and I was fortunate to have had the training.

There was one hurdle remaining, the Board exams which consisted of three assessments: practical (embalming), objective (multiple choice) and subjective (essay)

I was excited about getting back to school for our two-week consolidation. However, there was one more thing to look forward to, I had two weeks at home with my family. It was time to get reacquainted.

My girls were used to being alone and so they disappeared with their friends. My husband was working. I wandered around, enjoying the scent of early summer. My fishing rod came out of storage for the first time in two years. My daughters loved to roam the lakes with me and they dusted off their rods too.

The practical examination is conducted in Toronto. The examiners are licensed directors with a minimum of five years experience. Since there were so many students to examine, the Board of Funeral Service opted to start the practical examinations before consolidation. Apprentices in Toronto were asked if they wished to take the exam during that week. When the Board office called I let them know I was at home. However, given four hours notice I would be happy to come to Toronto that week. The person at the Board office was not optimistic, they themselves did not usually have that much notice from the examining funeral homes. I didn't mind, I was enjoying my vacation.

The first day of the Board exams, mid-morning, the phone rang. It was the Board office. Could I be in Toronto by 1 p.m.? They named the funeral home and the examiner and I knew my answer immediately. I could not have picked a better situation for the practical exam if I had tried.

They called the funeral home, asked if they would mind if I was a bit late, it was west of Toronto and I was on the east side of the province. It left me with three hours to do a four hour drive. The Board office called back to confirm I was good to go. A pleasant "good luck" from the Board person started me on a mad tear through the house. The dog ran for cover. Four minutes later I was in my funeral suit and heading out the door. My husband stepped in front of me.

"I can't believe my luck," I babbled. "One of the best prep rooms in Toronto and—"

"Drive carefully. Did you hear me? Don't do anything foolish."

"I won't," I promised, as he hugged me and wished me luck.

"Hey Dad!" I heard my eldest daughter yell. "Tell that crazy woman her keys are in the car." She had backed my car out for me and left the motor running.

"Good luck Mom," she said as I thanked her and said goodbye.

I hit the highway at 140 km/hr knowing full-well I was breaking the law and would lose points if I were stopped, not to mention a healthy fine. Getting there on time and safely was my only concern. I tried to mentally review what I should do once I started the exam, but my concentration was off. I put on some quiet music and enjoyed the trip.

At five minutes past one I pulled into the funeral home parking lot and pried my achy fingers off the wheel.

As I entered the building the receptionist came from behind her desk and extended her hand. "Hi," she said. "Welcome. You must be our student." She directed me to a washroom and the lounge and poured me a coffee.

"Your examiner will be down in a minute. Good luck!"

As I picked up the cup I shook so hard I spilled coffee on the table. I closed my eyes and took some deep breaths.

"Don't fall apart now," I chided myself. "You've worked hard for this moment."

The examiner strolled casually into the room and extended his hand. I rose to greet him, my face portraying a calmness I didn't quite yet feel. We chatted comfortably for several minutes. It was obvious he was leaving it up to me as to when I was ready to start and he knew I needed a few minutes to unwind from the drive. Finally, I was ready.

"I have three questions to ask you," I said. "First – do we have permission to embalm?"

Had I not asked that question it would have meant an automatic failure. Under the Act the consent must be in writing. In extenuating circumstances verbal consent is acceptable.

"Yes," he responded. "This funeral was prearranged."

"Thank you," I said. "Second, may I see the medical certificate of death?"

"Certainly. I'll get you a copy right away." He left the room, returning with the medical, which he placed in front of me.

The deceased was elderly and had died of cancer. The place of death was a hospital. There were no contributing factors listed, just the type of cancer. That did not tell me much. Was the final cause of death respiratory failure? If so, the blood could be clotted, affecting my choice of fluids. If it was pneumonia would the risk of purge increase? If there was pulmonary edema or hemorrhage then my treatment plan would vary.

Cancer was not the real cause of death, failure of the heart, lungs or one of the major organ is. Would there be metastases? Would there be jaundice? Incorrect fluid selection could cause serious embalming failure. I could not make any judgement calls until I examined the deceased.

"Third," I said. "Do we have the clothing?"

"Not yet," he replied. "We are expecting it shortly."

Clothing affects the choice of vessels for injection. Long sleeves and a high neck are ideal, incisions are hidden and IV bruises can be covered.

"Are you ready?" The examiner smiled as he and led the way to the preparation room. The room was empty except for the body shrouded on one of the tables. The examiner explained that we were not to be disturbed during the exam unless absolutely necessary. I had been in that prep room many times at all hours when I worked at the funeral directors service and knew it to be a busy place. All their calls had been diverted to their other chapels during the exam.

He showed me where the supplies were and fetched a lab coat and gloves. After I was appropriately attired, I turned to him.

"What do you expect from me?"

"Just explain what you are doing and why."

I worked carefully and gently. I disinfected the body and set the features, explaining my actions and choice of mouth closure. My mind was actively working trying to decide what choice of fluids to use. The brand of chemicals he showed me I had not seen before, although when I mentioned that to him he explained the indexes and properties.

"My idea of an ideal practical exam," I quipped, "was to ask for permission to embalm and not receive it. That would be an automatic pass would it not?"

He laughed. "It doesn't work that way."

I explained that I would use the carotid/jugular for injection and draining (a standard choice). The exam was just like lab at school, even the obvious had to be explained.

However, I could not find either vessel, there were too many tumours. He tried too, unsuccessfully. Placing the instruments on the table he turned to me.

"Now what?"

"Femoral," I replied. "There are no palpable tumours in the inguinal region. I will watch closely for distention, there will be extravascular pressure. There could be purging as well."

I chose a pre-injection at a low pressure and low rate of flow. I explained that the pre would act to expand and clear the vascular system, restore the pH of the body (rigor is acidic), and work as a diagnostic – short circuits would be evident.

A short circuit would necessitate a multipoint injection, and I suspected that would be a fait accompli. I elected to inject the pre on a closed system which would allow me to see if the jugular vein surfaced as it distended. That way I could open it for drainage instead of using a femoral drainage tube. That procedure was successful and I breathed a sigh of relief.

The rest of the exam proceeded uneventfully. There were a few interruptions, all staged. He left the room for five minutes, a tactic to see how far I would progress on my own. As I started terminal disinfection another director came in with the clothing.

"Hi!" was his happy greeting. Turning to the examiner he asked "So, how was the practical?"

"Like all my practicals," the examiner replied.

The director turned to me and grinned. "Well, that means you passed."

I looked at the examiner. "I thought you weren't allowed to tell me if I passed."

"He didn't," the director said. "I said it for him." And they both smiled at me.

I still had to complete the dressing and casketing. The examiner showed me his choice of cosmetic and watched to see how receptive I was to new ideas, all part of the exam. Since the casket had not arrived, we skipped that part of the procedure.

The entire examination took four hours. I thanked him and headed straight home, driving the speed limit, stopping only at a drive through for a bite to eat. At home I sought out my notes and I double-checked the cause of death.

Technically a pre-injection was contraindicated for the type of cancer the deceased had. I was lucky that I did not get into trouble, but it was a judgement call and I had learned during my apprenticeship to go with the best plan. Not all cases were textbook.

Returning to Humber for our two-week consolidation was exciting. I had never stayed in a residence before and it was not quite what I expected. When I checked in, the individual at the desk looked at my white hair and then at the program I was in.

"I think you might be happier on the top floor," she said, handing me a key. The open concept of the residence was pretty but it was really noisy. My room was small and cozy and I rather liked that I didn't have to share.

The common areas were full of chatting, happy young people. I checked out the washrooms. To my horror they were co-ed. Bathtubs, showers, toilets, all in stalls, but co-ed. I really didn't know what to do about that situation, I had no choice short of checking out and spending two weeks in a hotel. Financially, that wasn't going to happen. I learned to wait until the washroom was empty and prayed no one came in.

That didn't work of course. I never did get comfortable with the co-ed dorm concept.

I found a few of my classmates later that day in the cafeteria. As more showed up we shared stories of triumphs and failures and laughed at one another's mistakes. One of the girls told of cutting a director's jacket up the back, mistaking it for the deceased's jacket. It was the directors fault, he had laid it over the clothing she was fitting while he assisted with casketing another body.

Another classmate had a knack for fender benders with the limo and funeral coach. She had earned the nickname 'Crash'. We talked about the sadness and tragedy we had encountered on the job. It was a different group from two years prior, more mature and confident. Of the one hundred and thirty-five who had started first year, seventy of us were left. In a few weeks, fifty would be licensed with the other twenty rewriting in six months.

On the first morning of class, the Registrar from the Board of Funeral Services spoke to. She mentioned that forty percent of the newly licensed directors in Ontario (us) would be before the Board for a complaint or disciplinary action at some point in our career. We were the first class to be licensed under the new Funeral Directors and Establishments Act. We were also told that a Board representative would be conducting interviews with each of us to ask how our apprenticeships had gone and to listen to our suggestions.

One of the regulations under the new Act was that the apprenticing student conduct five at-need and five pre-need arrangements. Quite a few students had not completed that requirement, their employers did not want a student working with families. That made very little sense, one day you were a student, the next day you were a licensed funeral director and expected to assume all the duties and responsibilities that entailed. One of the managers of one of the largest funeral homes in the province had stated clearly to the Board that if the regulations forced him to allow students to conduct arrangements, then his funeral home would not take students.

"What a shame," I thought to myself. "They will lose their poorly paid gophers." After class it was the topic of discussion, the pay rate for apprentices was different around the province and those of us in Toronto were very fortunate compared to our country and small town classmates.

The Registrar also outlined what the examinations would entail. Ninety percent of the subjective exam was on pre and at-need contracts and legislation. The students who had not had the opportunity to arrange funerals were at a distinct disadvantage. Some of their employers had offered to do a mock arrangement with them. Every one of them who had been in that situation had declined. It was an insult to their intelligence.

Some directors still persisted in maintaining the mystique – only a licensed director should know what's going on. So much for teamwork. It showed a serious lack of respect on their part and a lack of education, they did not want the changes the new Act was bringing to Funeral Service. Board inspectors would be visiting those funeral homes in the not too distant future.

There are times when you can't legislate morality. Some of the female students were nothing more than assistants, cleaning the funeral home and working visitations. They did the required number of preparations but that was all. I had the utmost respect for them, sticking it out when their counterparts, like me, were receiving the best training possible. It wasn't fair, but it showed their commitment to their chosen profession.

A representative from the professional association also spoke to us and encouraged us to join. During our in-service year we were given honorary memberships. The Ontario Funeral Service Association has a number of committees that are actively working with the government, consumers, and agencies to keep the licensed directors in the province informed about such issues as disaster planning, changes in the legislation of the fourteen acts that govern funeral service, public awareness, labour relations, pay equity, human rights and environmental issues as they pertain to funeral service.

We also had our graduation photos taken that day. It was quite a thrill to don the burgundy gown and gold sash and feel the sense of accomplishment.

The afternoon was devoted to an objective examination designed to give us an idea of where we stood in relation to the pending Board exams. Sixty-five was a pass. Our marks ranged from forty-four percent to eight-five percent with the majority hovering around sixty percent. That was enough to jolt us into settling down, no parties or goofing off. There would be time enough to celebrate after Boards. We did arrange for an evening volley ball game at the residence, taking an hour off to socialize and let off steam.

The out of town students were scheduled for their practical exams during the two week period. It was quite an adventure for them just finding the examining funeral homes. For a student who had apprenticed in a small town, Toronto was a nice place to visit, just not to drive around. Those of us who knew the city did our best to help out by driving them to their exam between classes, drawing maps of the subway and transit system or lending our cars when we couldn't get away.

The time spent in class was a condensed version of each course, we covered a semester in two hours. Suggestions such as 'in past years the Board has been known to examine on this…' or 'The Board tends to look at this issue because of the media attention' were clues to study up. With almost four hundred million dollars in trust funds for prearranged funeral we could expect a thorough examination of the legislation.

The switch from the Ministry of Health to the Ministry of Consumer and Commercial Relations caused the focus to change from allied health care to consumer and contracts. It explained why some of the students had not received the training they deserved in their apprenticeships. Their bosses had completed their training at the Canadian School of Embalming, established in 1937 at the Banting Institute. It wasn't until 1968 that Humber took over the training of funeral service students.

Legislation continued to change the direction of funeral service. Change is hard and some funeral directors didn't like it, not understanding the need for a two-year program. Having worked with a few old-school directors only a couple were rigid in their dislike of rules and legislation that opened the door for the consumers' right to know.

One of our classmates had been involved in removing and preparing bodies after a disaster in her area. Several of the victims were children. For three days and nights the funeral home staff worked nonstop to prepare the bodies for shipment. Some of the remains had been mutilated beyond recognition. When she stopped working she slept for twenty-four hours and did not get out of bed for two days. Nightmares haunted her for weeks in spite of a debriefing from a police psychologist called in to work with the first responders. There was no question she had been irreparably changed by the experience. She had a quiet maturity and gentleness about her. As she shared her story we were deeply moved.

When a disaster occurs and many lives are lost, it falls on the coroner, pathologists and funeral directors to make sense of the mess and assist the families of the victims. One of the most gratify tasks a funeral director can do is to make it possible for the survivors to view the body. The shock of a sudden death, when a loved one was happy and healthy hours before, is life changing. The fear of what happened to the one they love and not knowing can be worse than the reality. Seeing is believing and it can be the beginning of the grief process and closure.

We asked her if she had considered giving up funeral service as a career. She admitted that there were moments when she thought of it. She said that when they'd completed restoration of the bodies that could be salvaged and she saw how it affected the families when they came to identify their relatives, she knew she wouldn't quit.

The day of the Board exams was bright and sunny. We wished each other good luck and settled into the first exam: two hundred and fifty multiple choice questions. It was a quiet bunch that left after it was over.

The following morning, we wrote the subjective exam: short answers and essay questions. During our group study, we had speculated as to what might be on that exam. We had not counted on the length of it, eleven pages of questions with a time limit of two and half hours.

We all glanced frequently at the clock, knowing we were losing the race. At the end of the two and a half hours the Board officials realized they had to extend the time, not one student had left the room. An hour later, I left with the rest of my class wishing I had another hour. It had been brutal. My answers were choppy and hastily written. I had not been able to proof or edit to my satisfaction. Several students left the room in tears and we did our best to console them. As it turned out, one quarter of the class failed that exam and it had to be put on a bell curve to raise the marks.

If a student failed any one of the three components of the Board exam they could rewrite in six months. Two attempts were allowed and if they were unsuccessful they could repeat the two years at Humber.

Having written the exam we, in effect, had graduated from the funeral service program at Humber. The dinner and dance was that evening and the party started early in residence. The following day was convocation where we would accept our diplomas.

None of my family were able to attend. It was enough for me that they had supported me through the tough two and a half years. I was with my classmates, some for the last time. Funeral directors tend to burn out early in their careers, moving on to less stressful work. The average "lifespan" of a funeral director is five years so I knew I would not see many of them at post-grad five years later.

We posed for a group photo for the national funeral publications. I didn't stay for the reception. The lump in my throat and the tears were making the good-byes difficult. I sought out John, Don, Paul and Ward to thank them and say good-bye. After walking quickly to my car, I headed home.

The results of the Board exams were to be mailed out in three weeks. I devoted myself to continuing my job search, a discouraging task. Outside Toronto it was difficult to get an interview because I was female. The occasional funeral home was open about the fact that female directors would not be hired, one manager told me that his clients would not take kindly to a female director driving a funeral coach and leading a funeral.

As the three-week wait for the marks period approached, my daily trek to the mailbox was marked by anxiety. Each day my anticipation rose only to be dashed when the mail did not yield the letter. Four weeks after exams I called one of my classmates who was working in Toronto to see if she had received her results. She said that the rumours were that the Board had marked the exams and were concerned about the high failure rate.

Neither of us wanted to wait so she called the Board office. They had nothing to say except that they hoped to mail the results the following week. I did my best to fill the time, my mind mostly on whether or not I'd passed.

About a week later my husband returned from the mailbox and handed me a letter. It was another rejection from a job application. I tossed it aside with a sigh. Seven months of job hunting and still nothing. I was running out of province, there were not a lot of funeral homes left to apply to.

"By the way, you might want to read this," he said, pulling a letter marked "Board of Funeral Services" from his pocket.

I panicked. "I can't open it. I just can't. You do it."

He laughed at my three-alarm dither and took his time opening the envelope and unfolding the contents. He then stood there making little sounds of hmmm, uh-oh, etc. until I snatched it from his hands. By that time the rest of the family was standing around, even the dog, who sensed something was up.

I scanned the pages trying to take it in.

"You made it," my husband announced and we all laughed. I headed to the phone to call some of my classmates. They too had passed and we laughed and cried together.

Would I do it again? I don't think so. It had taken too much from me. I was now free to indulge in reading a book for pure enjoyment, puttering through the mall with no timeline. I was also free, should I find a job, to enjoy my work, to spend time with families and assign and delegate some of the tasks to the support staff.

I was licenced.

When my licence arrived I framed it, along with this poem my sister cross-stitched for me. The author is unknown.

THE UNDERTAKER

The midnight hour, the darkest hour
That human grief may know,
Sends forth its hurried summons...bids me to come.
-I go-
I know not when the bell may toll,
I know not where the blow may fall
I only know that I must go in answer to the call.
Perhaps a friend...perhaps unknown...
'tis fate that turns the wheel.
Our tangled web of human life
Winds slowly on the reel.
And I! I'm the Undertaker
"Cold blooded," you'll hear them say,
"Trained to the shock and chill of death...
With a heart that's cold and grey..."
Trained...that's what they call it...

How little they know the rest.
I'm human and know the sorrow
That throbs in the human breast.

CHAPTER THIRTEEN

Blessed are They Who Mourn

"Mourning is not forgetting," he said gently, his helplessness vanishing and his voice becoming wise. "It is an undoing. Every minute tie has to untie and something permanent and valuable be recovered and assimilated from the knot. The end is gain, of course. Blessed are they that mourn, for they shall be made strong, in fact. But the process is like all human births, painful and long and dangerous."

-*The Tiger in the Smoke*

Margery Allingham 1957

The cameraman adjusted his lighting.

"Now, don't move. Try to hold the position you're in. You can move your hands when you talk though."

I braced my feet on the floor and hid my hands under the desk, trying to control my discomfort.

"What questions do you plan to ask?"

"I never give out my questions ahead of time," the interviewer responded as he picked up the microphone and turned to his cameraman. "Are we ready?" he asked.

"Yep."

"Exactly what is the difference between a transfer service and a funeral home?"

The microphone was diverted to my side of the desk awaiting my reply.

I took a breath in and began to answer. And so it went, for half an hour. After the interview was completed, various shots were taken of the office of the interviewing, and me looking at the urns, cardboard container, and the lone wooden, very plain casket.

Ten days before I had opened the transfer service. Six weeks before, opening this business would have been inconceivable. I had expected to get a job as a funeral director somewhere in the province. I made use of the time to start some post graduate training from the U.S., working on a Thanatology course and Infectious Embalming course in order to complete a CFSP designation. (Certified Funeral Service Practitioner). The designation had no weight in Canada but it was interesting and I enjoyed the studying.

A year after graduating, my job search had been unsuccessful. I had applied to every corner of the province, including a town so far north there were no roads in. Transportation in and out was by plane. Ground transportation was by ATV and snowmobile.

When a funeral director in my area called me to see if I would manage a transfer service for him, I was reasonably open to the idea. We discussed our philosophy of funeral service. Although I tend to think of funerals as traditional, my time in Toronto taught me that as a multicultural society not everyone will avail themselves of a "traditional" funeral. Funeral homes offer direct cremation and burial, but not everyone was comfortable using a funeral home for those services.

During our discussion, it was clear that the owner would give me free rein – I could take the time to work with the families I was servicing.

The interview was the only way I had of addressing some of the opposition from the area funeral homes. A small group had approached the suppliers threatening to cut them off if they provided the transfer service with urns and containers. The economic pressure was successful and we had lost some suppliers. It did open the door for independent urn makers to approach us, a beneficial alternative for both of us, as they were artists and their work was beautiful.

The crematorium and cemetery managers were being pressured to shut us out or raise the price of cremation for us alone. That did not work, regulations for cemeteries and crematoriums were in place.

With some trepidation, we had price advertised. In a conservative city this was not well received by some funeral homes. However, lawyers had experienced the same pressure from their peers when they price advertised. The end result had been positive, it benefitted the lawyer and consumer. Consumers were more likely to seek legal advice when they saw the bottom line, it was often less then they expected.

Our price advertising was a major bone of contention. One angry funeral home owner in a letter-to-the-editor stated that the consumer would only misinterpret the price advertising.

At no time did I criticize the area funeral homes. I made a point of explaining to people who enquired about our services that funeral homes do offer value for the services they perform, and that funeral homes have always offered direct cremation and burial. If during an arrangement conference I sense the family wanted to view the deceased, I would immediately refer them to a funeral home.

Some of the funeral directors, to their credit, ignored the rumours that were flying around and came in to see me. They were open enough to face the perceived problem and confront it. In reality the transfer service was not a threat to any one funeral home, or for that matter, to all of them collectively.

Under the funeral Directors and Establishments Act a transfer service does not have to be managed by a licensed funeral director. The regulations do place restrictions on transfer services such as no preparation of the body, and no identification (viewing) of the body can take place once the body has been transferred. The staff cannot attend a graveside, church/chapel or memorial service. The price for direct cremations/burial is low only because we did not have the facilities a funeral home could offer. Our overhead was low.

When a family chooses a transfer service they may be looking for several things, a quick direct burial or cremation and/or an opportunity to manage their own memorialization. They may be on a restricted budget or respecting the wishes of the deceased. Whatever the reason, funerals are for the living and there was room for involvement on their part. I did my best to help them find meaningful and creative ways to celebrate the life of the deceased.

After reviewing the options with the family, and if they wished to proceed with direct disposition, my job was done other than to transfer the deceased to the crematorium and cemetery.

Clergy had also approached me, willing to assist families who had not attended church for a while who wanted a service. They were willing to take the urn into their church and minister to the family, no follow-up if the family did not want it.

One of my early clients, a young widow, handed me a tiny porcelain elephant to put in the container with her husband. It had special significance for the two of them. I didn't ask why, or what. I simply placed the little elephant in his hand and closed the lid.

Scattering of cremated remains was the choice for the majority of families. During an arrangement conference I would take the time to explain the long term implications of scattering. In Ontario cremated remains can be scattered anywhere except Crown Land. They will scatter the cremated remains where they want and who is looking if they encroach on Crown Land?

However, scattering all the cremated remains may not be the best idea for a family. Unfinished business and a sense of loss can occur six months or so after the scattering has taken place. There are a lot of empty niches in cemeteries because grieving families needed a place to memorialize long after the scattering took place.

Recommendations such as scattering part of the cremated remains and waiting three to six months before scattering the rest often goes unheard. The family wants to carry out the deceased's wishes to be scattered, and their inclination is to do it quickly and put it behind them. Approximately eighty percent of families who scatter keep the container that held the cremated remains, even if it is just the plastic or tin box provided by the crematorium. That in itself speaks volumes – parting with their loved one was not as painless as they thought it would be.

In order to maintain my licence, I was required to work a minimum of fifteen hours a weeks in a funeral home as a director, giving me the opportunity to maintain and improve the technical skills I acquired during my training.

I was on call twenty-four hours a day, three hundred and fifty-one days a year at the transfer service. The funeral home manager who owned the transfer service did not want or need a female director, so the agreement was that I would not do traditional funeral arrangements.

Infectious embalming was an area where I felt useful at the funeral home, most of my colleagues were reluctant to prepare an infectious body. A funeral home manager cannot force any employee to work with infectious remains. If a funeral director lacks the technical expertise, fair enough. But refusing to research and learn and remain open minded did not sit well with me.

I had one family cry with relief when I agreed to embalm their loved one. They had approached other funeral homes only to be told the casket had to be closed because the body was infectious. That was not a solution, it was an excuse not to serve them.

The day I stop learning and growing is the day I need to get out of funeral service. The enjoyment and fulfilment I receive from this profession surprises me still. It's a privilege to serve and humbling to watch a family struggle with courage and dignity, with the pain of grief. As a director, I learned daily about our humanity and frailty from observing each family's journey.

CHAPTER FOURTEEN

The Repatriation of Cathy

Unlike previous chapters, this chapter is written from a personal relationship with the family and with their permission. I wrote the majority of this book from the perspective as a funeral director. My first responsibility was to a bereaved family. Emotional involvement clutters professional judgement, in this situation it was hard not to become emotionally involved.

The call came in on a busy morning at the funeral home. I picked up the line. In a voice choked with sobs, my brother-in-law in Toronto told me that his seventeen-year-old niece, Cathy, had died while on vacation in Cuba. She and her mom Carol lived in our city. Her father, Doug, and brother, Chris, also lived here. Carol and Doug were divorced.

"Please, call Carol and tell her you will help," he asked.

"I can't, Paul," I replied as gently as I could in a voice matching his. "It's not ethical."

“Please do something,” he said. He hung up.

I was stunned. Cathy and my girls had played together since they were little. I could not call Carol as a funeral director, but I could call her as a relative and as a mother. With trembling hands, I dialed her number.

“I am so sorry Carol,” I remember saying. “I am so, so sorry.” We cried together and talked briefly.

One of the staff was standing nearby when I hung up. He enveloped me in a hug and I buried my head on his shoulder. The hug from him was comforting and thoughtful.

Paul called again about twenty minutes later.

“I am at the transfer service. You’ll have to move fast. The next flight out of Cuba is two days from now. The transfer needs the Statement of Death information in the next two hours.”

“Paul, listen to me,” I said firmly. “Until the family calls and asks for our services I cannot help you. This has nothing to do with me until I hear from them that they will be contracting our services.”

“I’ll phone Carol right away,’ Paul said. “I want you to take care of things.”

Again, I was firm with him. "It's not your decision to make Paul, it is Carol's. I don't want her pressured in any way." Paul could not be dissuaded. It was his sister and they were close. I had done my best.

As soon as he hung up, Paul called Carol. Carol's initial reaction had been to book the first flight to Cuba. What mother wouldn't? Paul handed the phone over to the manager of the transfer service who told her that going to Cuba was the worst thing to do, the government would probably not let her see Cathy. The transfer service was not sure where in the country she was, and if Carol did go down there would be nothing she could do. He suggested she call a funeral home to start making arrangements and assured her that everything possible that could be done would be done.

Cathy was on March break and had gone to Cuba with nine other students. She fell ill near the end of the trip. Her friends took her to the hospital where she was put in an isolation bed. The last picture her friends had of her, as they were being herded out of the hospital for the fight back to Canada, was of Cathy on a ventilator being cared for by two nurses. Their pleas to stay with her fell on deaf ears. No one spoke English. The teenagers were escorted to the airport, still protesting, but to no avail. When the captain of the flight heard that he had passengers on board who had been exposed to meningitis he refused to take off. The Cuban government intervened and ordered the plane out of the country. The Ministry of Health in Canada was notified.

Meningococcal bacteria is virulent. It affects only a small number of people who have been exposed. Teenagers are particularly susceptible. The incubation period is two to ten days. Cathy had been in Cuba seven days when she became ill.

She could have contract the disease in Canada or Cuba. Had she fallen ill in Canada her chance of survival would have been as poor as it was in Cuba. In Canada no embalming would be allowed. the Medical Officer of Health has jurisdiction in such cases and can order immediate burial or cremation. The body must be placed in a hermetically sealed casket or metal sealer.

About ten minutes after Carol talked with the manager of the transfer service in Toronto, she called and asked to speak with me.

"Can you take care of things?" she asked. Her voice was flat. She was numb with grief.

“Of course,” I replied. “We need to get together as soon as possible.”

“Will tomorrow be soon enough?” Carol asked. I took a deep breath.

“I’m sorry, hon,” I said as gently as I could. “I don’t want to push you, but we should get together in the next few hours. We want to bring Cathy home.”

Up to this point Carol had received very little information. Just three hours before, a policeman had knocked on her door to tell her that her daughter was dead. She had known that Cathy had not disembarked with her friends at Pearson airport in Toronto the night before. My sister Penny had been waiting at the airport to pick Cathy up.

Her friends, upon disembarking had been taken away by the Ministry of Health to be treated with prophylactic antibiotics. They had thought Cathy would be home in a few days, her old self. They were able to tell Carol some of the story, what little they knew. The teens were exhausted and traumatized by the series of events leading to their departure from Cuba.

The family arrived with their priest. Carol took one look at me and with an anguished wail said, "I don't want to be here."

"I know Carol, I know," I said softly. We held each other for several minutes.

The manager was to have joined us during the arrangements. It was his funeral home, and his policy about female involvement held. Events around the funeral home precluded his attendance, however.

I proceeded without him, conscious of the need to answer Carol's questions, get the process started and make it as stress-free as possible for her. My experience with repatriation had taught me not to expect too much too quickly. Repatriation is subject to multiple international and national bureaucratic channels and snags. My main concern was to complete the vital statistics information required in the next few hours by the transfer service and to orient the family as to what they could expect over the next few days.

The air was heavy with grief and I took my time gathering the information. All of us were numb with shock – the body's 'time out' way of protection against situations too horrible to face.

At that point we knew Cathy had died of meningitis but not the exact strain. My clinical interest in infectious embalming meant that getting Cathy home quickly might mean the family could have a traditional funeral. Would the Cuban government allow her to be embalmed there? Would they just ship her home? There was nothing at that point in time to indicate that she could not be on the plane home in two days, or that she would be in a sealer (a soldered lead liner).

The worst nightmare faced by a parent is the death of their child. Compound that with the death occurring in a third world communist country. Fax machines were non-existent, telecommunication tenuous at best, transportation links were poor. The challenges mounted as one took into consideration the bureaucracy of a foreign government.

Canadian bureaucracy was complicated enough. The funeral directors service, acting as our agent, had started working with the Department of External Affairs, the Canadian consulate in Cuba (federal) and the Ministry of Health (provincial). On a district basis the Medical Officer of Health was required to go through the provincial office. Those officials did not work weekends and it was already Thursday.

I suggested that the family set their phone to have their answering machine on, turn off the volume, and have someone screen the calls. The media had begun to pick up the story and it had gone national. The press notice was prepared and would go into the local paper quickly, stating that funeral arrangements were incomplete and to call the funeral home for further information.

A scholarship fund in Cathy's name was being set up and memorial donations designated to it. Out of town family could be housed in hotels in town, in order to avoid additional strain on the immediate family. Penny and Paul and their kids would stay at my place. A spokesperson for the family was appointed to handle the media. As a funeral director, I did not deal with the media. I referred them to the family spokesperson.

After sending the family home with the promise to keep them informed about every evolving detail, I took a few minutes alone in the lounge to reflect. I had given the family my pager number, they had my home number, and I'd told them to call anytime. As soon as I could get away I went home to break the news to my daughter.

My oldest daughter had lost several friends in the past year. Cathy's death was very upsetting to her. She was very quiet over the next few days but also very helpful. My time at home with Paul and Penny was minimal and my daughter stepped up, running errands, cleaning, helping prepare meals and supporting her cousins in their grief. I was very proud of her. She had come a long way in the few years since her initial response to funeral service.

The next few days were spent on the phone, working with the transfer service and answering dozens of inquiries about the funeral. Tentative arrangements were made for visitation in three days. The first evening was reserved for family and friends and was not put in the press notice. The following day, a Monday, was a public visitation with the service to be held at the cathedral Tuesday morning.

Cathy's school was quick to respond. One of the teachers met with me to co-ordinate the visitation. I was asked to be part of the support team at the school when the students were notified of her death.

It has been said that sixty percent of people become ill after a death. I had always taken that to mean immediate family. In this case I hadn't counted on it being staff. The manager was the first to become ill. Normally most of us would push through an illness and keep working, but this bout of influenza knocked him off his feet. It had been years since he missed a day due to illness.

As Friday drew to a close, the phones at the funeral home started to get busy. For the most part people were reasonable when informed that the arrangements were incomplete and to please check back Sunday.

About the only time I felt any annoyance or frustration was when someone who called wasn't satisfied with our answer. Remarks such as "what do you mean incomplete, where is Cathy now, when is she coming home" or "why can't you tell me", were met with a quiet resistance on my part. Unless they were family, no one needed to know.

Some people were annoyed that the family wasn't answering their phone. Setting the phone on answering machine and turning off the volume had been a good idea, it rang nonstop for days.

Any official information about Cathy's repatriation would come through the funeral home via the transfer service. Sadly one of the screened calls was a death threat and the police were informed. By Friday evening the transfer service was able to let us know for sure that Cathy would not be leaving Cuba that weekend. The next available flight was the following Wednesday. I met with the family to notify them of the change of plans. A decision had to be made about the visitation and service.

I hated to approach them with nothing definite. The transfer service had informed us they were not sure Cathy would be on the fight the following Wednesday. All that was known at that point was a metal sealer had been used. That was the most devastating blow of all, she could not be embalmed, nor could there be an open casket.

The family made the choice to go ahead with visitation and a memorial service with a private graveside service when Cathy came home. That meant I could update the press notice for Saturday's paper, the details of the service and visiting now available. In spite of the updates the phones at the funeral home rang constantly.

The next illness was my sister Penny. She arrived at our home late Saturday evening. I had just come in the door, my days were quite long since the funeral home had several other calls, the manager was off, and the phones were busy. I still had the transfer service to run.

Penny's asthma was acting up. She'd taken the usual bronchodilators without result. As her voice faded and she started experiencing chest pain I suggested we go to the hospital. It was a seventy-five-kilometer drive, but from experience I knew asthma and funerals didn't mix.

As I was getting ready she started complaining of nausea. Chest pain, shortness of breath, nausea, I looked at my husband. He nodded and called an ambulance. Their response time was thirty minutes, a tense wait but at least they had oxygen. She wasn't happy about the ambulance but her protests fell on deaf ears.

As it turned out, it was a heart problem. She required nitroglycerin and oxygen to relieve the pain. She did not want to spend the night in hospital and went against medical advice once she was pain free and breathing better. The doctor pulled me aside and gave me a stern warning to bring her back immediately if there was even a small change and definitely in six hours regardless. As we left he reinforced his warning with the comment, "I don't want to hear this woman has had a heart attack in the morning."

The private visitation Sunday evening was attended by several hundred people. We knew that the students and their families from Cathy's school would require overflow management, so we expanded the visitation Sunday evening at Carols' request to accommodate as many as possible. People were asked to take a seat in the chapel as the visitation rooms filled. Mementos and collages were placed among the flower arrangements. Cathy had accomplished quite a lot for a seventeen-year-old girl. One of the pictures on a collage showed her with her cousins and my girls. I avoided looking at the photo each time I walked by.

One of the staff members wasn't feeling well. As visitation wound down he collapsed in the chapel. I was close enough to break his fall. I decided to drive him home. He called a little later to say he was worse and was going to the Emergency ward.

As soon as I closed the funeral home, I went to the hospital to look for him and found him flat on his back with an IV running. He had the flu and his blood sugar was too high. Two trips to the hospital in two days. My sister was still in bed, the manager hadn't even checked in.

Early Monday morning I arrived at the high school. I had elected to wear my funeral suit. I did not want to intimidate any students who might want to approach with questions, but this situation was real. Many students had not dealt with a funeral director before, nor been to a funeral home. I had also asked the staff who had funeral suits to wear them on duty for Cathy's visitation.

The first order of business was a staff meeting. The psychologist and I were introduced. I brought the staff up to speed as to what was happening with the visitation and service, explained that Cathy was still in Cuba and the service was now a memorial service.

At nine a.m. the principal opened the announcements with the news of Cathy's death. The school priest led the students and faculty in prayer. Rooms had been set aside for students to gather for coffee and support. I was struck by the spiritual atmosphere of the school – many of the students headed straight for the chapel. At ten a.m. the school stopped again for prayer. In the classroom I was in, the students talked openly about their feelings. I answered their questions honestly. Most had seen the national news reports. The staff was supportive and kind. A memorial book was put out so the students could write their thoughts and memories of Cathy for her family.

The school had taken a proactive approach to Cathy's death. Several years before they had experienced a similar situation and had learned from it. During visitation at the funeral home that afternoon they booked a public school gym across the street and positioned teachers outside the funeral home to direct students through in controlled groups.

Local businesses had donated refreshments. Teachers were on hand in the gym to lend support. The principal kept vigil with the other teachers during visitation, watching for students who might be experiencing difficulty. The presence of the teachers made the funeral home staff members' jobs much easier. Hundreds of students filed through the funeral home that day. Through it all Carol and Doug remained gracious and calm. I don't know how they did it.

With all that was going on, it had not occurred to me that the manager would not be well enough to take his place as lead director for the service the next morning. He called early Tuesday morning to tell me he couldn't make it. The other director had his own funeral that day. I called a staff meeting and briefed what few staff were left and asked for their opinions and advice. The lead limo driver was to arrive at the family's home fifteen minutes early. The other two drivers were to pick up passengers at several locations around the city. They arrived only to find no one there. I was at the cathedral setting up.

When the lead limo arrived at the house, no one was dressed. That was quite understandable. For two days they'd greeted hundreds of people. They were physically and emotionally spent. The service was one more hurdle in their grief. The early arrival was timed in case they weren't ready and served as a motivator.

Some of our wayward passengers were at the house.

"Maybe we should have called and told you we were coming here, we changed our minds at the last minute," one of them said me over the phone. I responded with a wry smile. Somewhere in the city I had two cars out and about with no way to reach the drivers. We had thirty minutes to round everyone up. I reassured them it was all good and retreated to my car to sit and wait. I had absolute faith in the staff and figured it would work out. It did.

We were to rendezvous at the funeral home and drive in procession to the cathedral. As I pulled up to the funeral home, two limos were waiting. The family limo arrived a couple of minutes later and proceeded to the cathedral, right on time.

As I helped the family out of the car I didn't even glance around to look for media. My thoughts were on the service and the seating.

As we entered the cathedral I nodded to the priest that we were ready. He looked rather puzzled. Nothing happened. He kept looking around and it dawned on me. I forgot for a minute that it was because I was female. He was used to our manager or the other director and I finally had to approach him.

"The manager is off sick, we are ready to proceed when you are," I said quietly and stepped back.

The cathedral seated over twelve hundred and it was full. The high school choir was singing. I seated the nearly thirty family members, including my husband and girls and after genuflecting, took my seat on the right

The service was incredible. There were nine priests and a protestant minister. It was deeply moving. One of Cathy's classmates, a gifted violinist, played Ava Maria during the Eucharist (Communion). I could feel the sobs well from deep inside. Grief is particularly susceptible to sound and the violin released mine. One of our staff handed me a Kleenex. He should have kept it for himself, there wasn't a dry eye in the cathedral.

As I led the family out, Carol took my arm. We squeezed other's hand. I glanced around and saw the media wolf pack.

"Let's get you into the limo quickly," I said. "You can greet people at the reception. She agreed. Twelve hundred people had attended the service at the cathedral and greeting them on the street would be impossible.

I left the cathedral and returned to the funeral home. The funeral directors service called while I was out to inform me that Cathy would not be on the flight the next day. Her luggage would be, but Customs would be confiscating it as a biohazard. I decided not to tell Carol until after the reception, there was no point adding to her stress.

Meanwhile, I had the transfer service to run and families to serve. The rest of the week was busy. Carol and Doug were never far from my thoughts. Until Cathy was back on Canadian soil my job was not done.

Friday I called to suggest they go to the cemetery to purchase a plot. The cemetery made arrangements to have the grave opened Monday just in case Cathy was on the Saturday flight. It had been almost two weeks. Our agents were not too sure where Cathy was located, she could have been in Havana or on the far side of the island.

New regulations in Cuba required all repatriations take place out of Havana. Cathy was booked to come home on Saturday's flight. I made plans to drive to Toronto Saturday evening to pick her up, pending confirmation from the transfer service.

Friday the flu hit me with a vengeance. I crawled into bed early, willing it to go away.

Several times Saturday I heard from the service. I had no plans to leave for Toronto until the plane touched down at Pearson. Her flight was to land in Montreal where she would be transferred to an Air Canada commuter flight to Toronto. It would take a while to clear customs in Montreal.

I slept off and on all day Saturday as my temperature rose and fell.

Late Saturday afternoon our agents called to say that officials at Mirabel in Montreal were unable to locate Cathy. They were not impressed. Neither was I. We were not dealing with a piece of lost luggage.

That evening Cathy was located. She had not been put on the plane in Cuba. She was still in Havana.

All that evening the funeral directors service staff worked with an official from the Department of External Affairs. Permission was given to fly her out of Havana Sunday, and special clearance arranged so the Cuban plane could land at Pearson International in Toronto to offload her.

When the plane arrived Sunday, it had to stay on the taxiway, engines running. For a few tense moments no one would accept responsibility for the shipment. An Air Canada official rushed out to the plane just as it was getting ready to leave. Cathy nearly went to Montreal after all. It took only a few minutes for our agents to clear customs, the way had been paved by the Department of External Affairs.

I remember saying to someone at the funeral directors service that when the plane landed I would be the happiest funeral director in the province. I didn't feel happy. I was just glad she was home. The long ordeal was now over from a funeral director's point of view, but certainly not from the family's perspective. So many families are faced with repatriation. How does one prepare for the days of waiting, the uncertainties?

The service asked me if I wanted the air tray (the outer shipping container) opened. I gave permission since a funeral coach was being used and the casket would be sealed. I had checked with the Ministry of Health on the off chance that we might have permission to open the sealer. I could not be sure of what I would find, but I felt it was worth asking. Permission was denied. Meningococcal bacteria can be found in host tissue ten days post mortem. It was too risky.

I was just getting ready to leave for Toronto when my phone rang again. It was the funeral directors service.

"She's viewable," I was told.

"What? How?" I exclaimed.

Someone in Cuba had prepared (embalmed) Cathy and put a small glass viewing window in the sealer. We later surmised that the officials had ordered the preparation of the body. It would have had a negative effect on the tourist trade if things had not gone well. Canada and Cuba had good relations. Nonetheless, it was a very special gift that a pathologist gave Cathy's family. The doctor risked his or her life to do it. It was obvious that great care had been taken in her preparation.

I took someone with me to Toronto, I was feverish and achy. We arrived back at the funeral home late Sunday night. Carol, Doug and Chris arrived within minutes of my call. As hard as it was for them to see her, it would have been much, much harder not to.

All that remained was the graveside service. For her parents, their grief work was just beginning, many difficult months lay ahead. They were planning on attending a support group for bereaved parents. It has been said that grief shared is grief diminished. But as I said in Chapter One, no one can really know another's pain, only the person it affects can fully comprehend it.

From a funeral director's perspective, repatriation involves a great deal of effort and time. Not all such calls have positive outcomes like this one. Each is a learning experience and requires the best efforts of a number of people to facilitate the repatriation as quickly as possible in order to alleviate the family's stress.

Cathy was finally laid to rest two weeks after her death.

AFTERWORD

Hindsight is 20/20. I look back over the years and marvel at how fortunate I was to have worked in my chosen profession. I would do it again in a heartbeat.

Was it easy? No. I have been asked what advice I would give to someone thinking of entering the funeral profession now. Much has changed, cremation vs. burial, traditional vs. memorial services. Funeral costs are prohibitive for many. Funeral directors have had to become more flexible, more involved in facilitating a person's grief. Post graduate training in grief recovery is available to funeral service personnel.

If this is your true calling, get a well-rounded education. You'll be dealing with rich, poor, Ph.Ds, high school drop outs. Grief is no respector of persons. Learn as much as you can about other cultures. Read the news, read non-fiction *and* fiction. Never stop reading, never stop learning. The best funeral service students are the ones who have to try their best, who are willing to put the work in, and who never stop learning.

Be kind, be respectful.

Look after yourself. Understand and practice self-care, self-awareness, self-respect. Without them, you will burn out. Lean on your peers, help each other. If you're afraid of your emotions, then how can you help the families you serve?

For more information on funeral service and what funeral directors do, check the memoirs section of Amazon or other book sites. Visit the colleges in your country that offer funeral service education or ask your local funeral director.

I hope my memoir opened the door to the funeral home, the morgue (sorry – no zombies), the profession. Remember, when you shed tears of grief, it is likely your funeral director has been there too.

J. Richardson 2017

ABOUT THE AUTHOR

Born in Toronto, Canada, Jan has lived and worked in various parts of Ontario. Her original career choice was medical office assistant; her dream was to be a funeral director. Eventually she fulfilled that dream, and got her license. Jan's first book, The Making of a Funeral Director, is a non-fiction account of what funeral service education is really like.

Now Jan has settled in the Niagara Region as it's a great place to live, one never tires of the falls.

The Spencer Funeral Home Niagara series flows best if the books are read in order:

Book 1 Casket Cache
Book 2 Winter's Mourning
Book 3 Grave Mistake
Book 4 First Call

If you liked this book, please rate or review it – thank you!

You can find Jan on Twitter: @richardsonjan1, Facebook and Goodreads: Janice J. Richardson. She would be delighted to hear from you any time.